FINDING

"Joy embodies what it means to be a leader at home, at work, and in the world—all at the same time. Her courage, clarity, and commitment to make her unique contribution to a world that works are epic! Her book will both inspire and equip you to do the same."
—**Carolyn Buck Luce**,
Author of *EPIC! The Women's Power Play Book*

"Joy, a trailblazing corporate survivor, speaks life into the circumstances around her. She precisely measures her words to stimulate a thought-provoking reading experience."
—**Carolynn Johnson**, CEO, DiversityInc

"Joy's insights into how to effectively break barriers, smash glass ceilings and build lasting relationships, along with the stories of her personal and professional journey, provide a magical blueprint to help everyone truly achieve their authentic selves in the workplace."
—**Celeste Warren**, Vice President,
Global Diversity & Inclusion Center of Excellence, Merck

"In her own words…"That's REAL for me"…resonates from beginning to end as Joy masterfully pulls back the covers on today's experiences in corporate America. She shares insightful perspectives and speaks truth to power while providing practical tools that help us find our natural operating rhythms and unleash the full power of authenticity in navigating our careers."

—**Deena Rembert Neason**, VP, Global HR Operations

"This is unequivocally an amazing book. It is filled with insightful nuggets that one can utilize and put into action. It is the definitive guide for navigating the ins and outs of corporate America. Most importantly, I love how AUTHENTIC Joy is in her writing. I am just blown away. It's a must-read for sure!"

—**Dennis Kennedy**, CEO, Diversity First

"With the precision and passion of a truly authentic leader, Joy Fitzgerald provides the reader with practical tools and methodologies to not only find and live their purpose but also to live their truth daily with joy and happiness. Joy's empowering journey will surely touch every woman at every level."

—**Dr. Sheila Robinson**, Publisher & CEO,
Diversity Woman Media

"To those looking for the essential road map or how-to guide that provides readers with important insights for mastering who they are, while mastering a career in corporate America, pull up a chair and enjoy the incredible read by my respected friend Joy Fitzgerald. We all know that thriving in corporate America requires unique skills. However, finding your unique gifts, and offering them in corporate settings without compromise, can be very challenging – especially if you're a born positive disruptor. I've spent a large part of my career helping people develop, harness, and leverage the unique skills needed to maximize their career journey. So, I was pleased to discover *Finding Your Authentic Rhythm: How to Win on Your Terms in Corporate America* by Joy. What a gift and a reveal!"

—**Forest T. Harper Jr.**, President and CEO, INROADS, Inc.

"Great leaders know themselves and show themselves. In *Finding Authentic Rhythm*, Joy Fitzgerald has written a guidebook to help you do just that. Using relatable metaphors of music, she creates a powerful framework for personal and professional growth."

—**Gloria Feldt**, Cofounder and President of Take The Lead(R), Author of *Intentioning: Sex, Power, Pandemics, and How Women Will Take the Lead for (Everyone's) Good*

"With this invitation to explore our most authentic rhythm, Joy Fitzgerald shines a light on that critical but sometimes dark path towards self-knowledge and belief and reassures us it is the key to finding our purpose and having great impact in the world. Her generosity with her story and lessons will light a fire in every reader who picks up this book!"

—**Jennifer Brown**, Award-Winning Entrepreneur, DEI Consultant, Speaker, and Author of *Inclusion, Beyond Diversity, and How to be an Inclusive Leader*

"Joy answers the questions out loud that emerging leaders ask themselves silently. Her actionable advice turbo-charges the reader's confidence and ability to achieve success."

—**Joyce Brocaglia**, CEO,
Executive Women's Forum and Founder, Alta Associates

"I highly recommend *Finding Authentic Rhythm* for those navigating corporate America along any stage of their career journey. This book is an empowering read full of wisdom and insights that can teach women the confidence to discover and pursue their purpose, use their voice even when it's uncomfortable, and build relationship capital to advance their dreams. Share this book with all the women in your life so they can become the best version of themselves and achieve success on their own terms."

—**Johanna Zeilstra**, CEO, Gender Fair

"If you are living in the Rhythmless Nation of feeling stuck and lacking direction in your career…this book will get you back on track. Joy has a magical and mentoring way of infusing engaging stories from her remarkable corporate career while providing relevant and actionable advice that can be applied immediately. *Finding Authentic Rhythm* is an insider's guide on honing in on your own rhythm and finding flow in your career."

—**Joyel Crawford**, Author, Speaker, and Executive Coach

"Being an immigrant, working mother, and STEM leader in a male-dominated industry, my colleagues often told me that

I didn't fit into corporate America. It took some effort for me to have the balance and fight for myself. As I read this book, I found many answers to the challenges I have faced, and I see many women still facing them. I would recommend every woman to read this book. It is a handbook with practical examples to apply in many situations."

—**Rupal Thanawala**, CEO, Trident Systems

"*Finding Authentic Rhythm* took me on a journey that inspired and challenged me. It is a candid, vulnerable, and at times laugh-out-loud account of finding one's way in corporate America. Joy's tell-it-like-it-is writing style empowers individuals with the understanding needed to navigate the complexities of winning in corporate America and discovering one's authentic rhythm. This is a must-read for anyone who feels lost or is looking for a pathway to win on their terms."

—**Dr. Sheri Riley**, Award-Winning Author of *Exponential Living-Stop Spending 100% of Your Time on 10% of Who You Are*

FINDING AUTHENTIC RHYTHM

ALSO BY JOY FITZGERALD

*The Journey to Joy: 5 Generations Share
Stories Every Woman Needs to Hear*

*The Journal to Joy: Weekly Reflections to
Help You Experience More Self-Love,
Faith, and Happiness*

FINDING AUTHENTIC RHYTHM

How to Win on *YOUR* Terms in Corporate America

JOY FITZGERALD

Books may be purchased in bulk quantity and/or special sales by contacting the publisher.

Mynd Matters Publishing
715 Peachtree Street NE
Suites 100 & 200
Atlanta, GA 30308
www.myndmatterspublishing.com

978-1-957092-50-8 (pbk)
978-1-957092-51-5 (hdcv)
978-1-957092-52-2 (ebk)

FIRST EDITION

To my mother, Ann Phillips, you continue to believe in my dreams more than I do. You are indeed my dream builder.

To my daughter, Taylor, thanks for your innovative ideas and creative genius.

To my son, Tyron, thanks for being a great listener and helping me to think differently.

To my wonderful husband, Tyron, thanks for challenging me and ensuring I never felt alone during this journey.

Contents

FOREWORD

Having managed more than a billion dollars in revenue for some of the world's largest media companies including CNN, A&E, The History Channel, The Weather Channel, and BET Networks/BET Her, I've had a career that many would dream of attaining. I've been a strategic force inside and outside the bounds of corporate America. I've held the title of CEO for Ebony and Jet and currently serve as the President of Multicultural Advertising at a major Media Group. If you were to read my resume or biography, you might imagine that I've had the perfect career journey. Quite the opposite, my journey has not been a crystal stair.

I too have experienced challenges, setbacks, and disappointment while working in corporate America. What you don't see on my resume is that on February 27, 2020, I was fired from a high-powered position in the media industry. This is a day I will never forget. I was humiliated, angry, and discouraged. I was at one of the lowest points in my professional journey. You might say that my rhythm and beat were off! So, what did I do? I looked in the mirror and asked myself the question every one of you reading this book will ask yourself at some point in your career, *"What is my purpose and how will I get there? "*

Are you ready to find your purpose and win on YOUR terms? Are you willing to live your most authentic life? To be rewarded for your hard work? To be aligned with your life's purpose even if you don't know how you are going to get there? If you answered yes, you are not alone. I too have been on this journey. Many people look at my life and don't understand the sacrifices I've made to reach the pinnacle of success. I have worked for some of the most powerful companies in the world while holding the title of wife, mother, board member, community activist, and author. That doesn't happen without me doing the work and finding my authentic rhythm. Whether you have been fired, stuck in a hopeless job, propelled to the top of your career, or want something different, all of these are periods in our lives where we get out of rhythm and need to get back on track.

It is amazing how life comes full circle, and we never know the impact one moment in time can make in helping others find their way and their rhythm. Several years ago, I had the opportunity to speak at a women's conference on my new book where Joy was in the audience. Little did I know that my presentation would serve as the catalyst to helping Joy ignite the plan for her first book, finding her publisher (we have the same publisher), and the two of us making a powerful connection.

Over the years, I've watched Joy Fitzgerald dance through the hallways of corporate America and master her rhythm. Her career as a Human Resource Executive and Chief Diversity, Equity, and Inclusion Officer has given her the roadmap to true success. Joy is a master of the game when it comes to people, policy, and purpose. Her life's work is the framework for the playlist to our success.

Joy's brilliance shines through every page as she lays out examples of how she found her voice even in the most uncomfortable and complex situations. She reminds us that those we meet throughout our careers can help build us up or represent barriers to delay our progress and growth. Just as our connection was a catalyst to help her ignite her dream, I hope this book is a catalyst for you.

I challenge you to hear the beat of the pages, flow into the rhythm, and without hesitation, dance into your almighty God-given purpose.

Michele Thornton Ghee,
Award-winning Corporate Executive & Business Leader

INTRODUCTION
Words Are Powerful

"Everything in the universe has a RHYTHM,
everything dances."
—Maya Angelou

Thank you for making an investment in your authentic rhythm. Your decision may be based upon the title, a recommendation from a colleague, or maybe you chose to take an adventure on a random selection. Maybe the title resonated with you as you are desperately wanting to understand how to win on YOUR terms in corporate America. Whatever your reason, you have purpose in exploring the words and ideas between the following pages.

Here I am again, sequestered in my office at the proclamation and requirement of my husband and two young adult children. Today feels scary but it also feels like the first step in fulfilling an amazing dream. I know this sounds crazy, but you will understand more about my journey soon. So, here we go…

As early as I can remember, I desired to write a book. I fell in love with reading and writing at a very young age. In the beginning, my passion for reading was somewhat forced by my mother as she was insistent on making me read weekly as a child. I quickly became enamored with the intellectual stimulation of exploring the world, people, places, things, and relationships through the prose of written language. I guess you can say it was love at first read. Even today, one of my favorite places to visit is the bookstore. There is something magical about wandering through aisles filled with thousands of stories and experiences just waiting to be explored.

What I love most about reading is that it removes the present tense. It whisks you away to a land of possibilities and forces you to redirect your mind to what's happening in the story. Well, that's the case when you find the right book. So, get ready to be intrigued and inspired to dance to your authentic rhythm and beat.

My first book was a pivotal coming-out moment. I wasn't bold enough to step out on my own and write my journey. Hence, I relied on the women in my life that I love the most, my four generations, to help share the journey with me. They made the process less daunting and more attainable. They held me accountable for completing the task at hand to WRITE THE BOOK. It was so much easier to take a publicly vulnerable step knowing my foundation, family, and tribe entered the audacious task with me. I was not alone.

It's been three years since we wrote *The Journey to Joy: Five Generations Share Stories Every Woman Needs to Hear,* and it, by far, has been one of my most proud accomplishments. It shares familial stories of our triumphs, blessings, miracles, and hardships. It is a living testament in honor of the matriarch of our family, my great-grandmother Charity Maples, who lived one week shy of 101 years of age.

The Journey to Joy: Five Generations Share Stories Every Woman Needs to Hear is our gift to current and future generations to come. It has been a blessing to share our experiences with others, and we are beyond grateful for all who have read our stories and offered their sentiments of gratitude.

I feel compelled to share a vulnerable moment. I spoke and manifested *Finding Authentic Rhythm* while on stage at the *Women of Power Conference* in Las Vegas in March of 2022. I spoke this into existence prior to writing one single word. As the Bible reads, *My tongue is the pen of a skillful writer (Psalm 45:1).* Words are so powerful!

I have often been told I am a masterful storyteller. I am frequently asked how I learned this skill or what courses I took to become a public speaker. The real answer is (drumroll)…it's a God-given talent that comes naturally. I wish I had a genius protocol or process for how I navigate this space, but I don't. Stories come to me as easily as walking. It's what I've always known how to do, and on this day, this gift walked me right into **Finding Authentic Rhythm.**

It was March 2022, almost two full years after the beginning of the Covid-19 pandemic, and it was my first time attending a large conference in person since most of the world had gone to virtual events. Let me set the stage. *Women of Power*, hosted by *Black Enterprise*, is one of my favorite conferences. I was excited to be one of the panelists and back to where I felt seen and loved. How amazing is that?

Many women, especially women of color, have experienced feeling less than enough, invisible, unheard, devalued, disrespected, marginalized, assaulted, unprotected, and dismissed. So have I. Throughout history, there have been very few things that have honored women of color or created the platform or stage to share our greatness, gifts, and honored our journeys. This is one event of the year that profoundly fills my Black Girl Magic cup. It is the only time I get to see over a thousand women that look like me who are CEOs and business owners *slaying it* in corporate America and nonprofit organizations. It is the one conference I prioritize to ensure I don't miss attending. It is a coming together of sisterhood, motherhood, and Boss Women who are proud to embrace their heritage.

So here I am on stage with three other fabulous queens who have broken glass ceilings in corporate America getting ready to share words of wisdom. The room was filled with over 700 women of all ages and walks of life. The Black Girl Magic aroma in the atmosphere was so intense, words fail to describe it. It felt amazing to be amidst successful, strong, resilient, and accomplished women of color. Likewise, it was refreshing to be out and around people since I had avoided large crowds for almost two years for fear of catching "corona."

I was humbled to have friends and colleagues from my previous and current organization in the audience supporting and cheering me on. Likewise, my daughter, and best friend were center of the room, sharing their expressions of love and support.

The panel moderator began introducing us, and as she read my bio, I heard phrases permeate the room.

"Go, Joy!
That's our Chief Diversity Officer.
Whoop Whoop!
Yasss Girl!"

As I sat on the stage, I took a moment to soak in all the love in the atmosphere. I was grateful to be called upon to share my wisdom and experiences. I was feeling great, and in my element. After the moderator finished asking questions of the panel, she opened the floor for questions from the audience. A young lady stood up and looked directly at me and said, "Joy, thanks so much for your words of encouragement. You talked about your *S.I.S You Got This* model. Where can we learn more about it?"

I answered, "Well, you will have to purchase the book. It's called *Finding My Authentic Rhythm*." The audience began to yell "Yes!" and started clapping and high-fiving one another. I got so caught up in the adoration and the moment that I said, "And it will be available later this year. Please stay tuned by following me @SpeakingJoy on social media to learn more about the book's launch date."

Oh crap! What the heck did I just do? And where did this title come from? I had no idea, but it felt right at the time. But wait, I haven't even started writing the book, and I just told over 700 women that I would have a book launched in less than SIX MONTHS. What in the world have I done, and why did I say this?

Breathe, Joy, breathe!

I am sitting on stage with the biggest smile on my face that one can see. But, on the inside, I felt like I was about to pass out. I just committed and manifested something that felt so right to my subconscious but totally ludicrous to my rational mind. And why did this proclamation seem so unrealistic? Where will I fit this in my overwhelming, overbooked, and outlandish schedule?

After we finished the panel, one by one, women excitedly

came up to me and asked, "Where can I buy the book, and when will it be released?" The more I responded to this line of questions, the more excited I became. Each time I uttered the words "Finding Authentic Rhythm," I became more confident in the need to share my experience with the world. I became convicted and in total submission to the calling on my life to write this book, and boy, do I have a story to tell.

Once I returned to my hotel room, my daughter Taylor looked at me and said, "Mom, you were terrific! I am so proud of you. I got tickled because I know you didn't mean to say you had a book coming out later this year. But it's okay. Just think of it like this, your purpose spoke through you because you were operating in your purpose. You manifested precisely what needed to be born out of you, and oh, by the way, that title is FIRE!

"Did you see how everyone roared and clapped when you shared the title? This moment is destined, so embrace it.

Well, mom, I guess you better start writing and quick!"

I immediately picked up my cell phone and texted my publisher.

"Hi, I think we need to meet soon because I just committed to writing a book on stage at this conference. I haven't even started writing. And by the way, can we make it happen by the end of the year?"

My publisher responded, "Well, that's one way to hold yourself accountable. Let's talk."

And just like that, *Finding Authentic Rhythm* was born.

What is This Book About?

Finding Authentic Rhythm will share principles, tools, and methodologies I have created throughout my career and experience to help others navigate and thrive. I will reveal many of the secrets to success in breaking barriers, dismantling concrete ceilings, building relationships that count, and achieving sponsorship to accelerate one's career.

I will share stories of my journey as a little Black girl growing up in the South and my experiences navigating corporate America. I will share my mistakes, successes, and learnings as I've climbed the corporate ladder. Today, I occupy an executive leadership role at a Fortune 5 company, and I am still learning, growing, and evolving.

The tools and techniques shared in this book offer a unique perspective on raw and real topics sharing truths few want to discuss as we navigate through our careers. Topics will include stifled authenticity, hardships, racism, biases, cultural disconnections, the unwritten rules of success and so much more as I found my authentic rhythm.

I commit to being open, honest, and most of all, vulnerable to help you in your journey of finding your rhythm. I will share uncomfortable stories highlighting what I've witnessed, lived, and experienced. For the sake of privacy, I have renamed the critical players. Regardless of the circumstance, I am thankful for each person who ultimately helped develop me into who I am today. But just know, you might be reading about yourself. And for that, I offer no apologies only gratitude as your challenges have made me better.

I want every reader to know that you are not alone. Your struggles are my struggles. Your struggles are your sisters' and brothers' struggles. Your challenges and disappointments are real and not an indication or indictment that you are not good enough. Quite the opposite, you are more than enough! The fact that you purchased this book speaks to your investment and belief that you desire growth and better opportunities.

Secondly, I want each of you to feel inspired and encouraged by my journey as I struggled to figure out how to be successful without compromising the very essence of who I am. Truth moment: I did compromise pieces and parts of myself (I will share more later in the book.). I feared that being me was too much, too bold, too authentic, and not safe. But keep reading, it gets better.

If you have ever been coached, mentored, sponsored, or given the following feedback:

- You are too direct.
- You are too bold.
- You are seen as a little too aggressive.
- You can be intimidating.
- You should try to act like one of the boys!
- You should probably smile to make yourself more approachable.
- You are too buttoned up.
- You must do more than everyone else to be successful.

- You have zero room to make a mistake.
- Your race is something people struggle with, so be careful.
- You should be grateful to be where you are because you are a unicorn.
- You represent all women or women of color, so don't fail!

Or

- Don't negotiate your salary.
- Don't go for that next big role if you have small children.
- Don't dream big!
- Don't show vulnerability.
- Don't ask for what you want.
- Don't speak up.
- Don't walk away if you are unhappy.

Then this book is FOR YOU!

I want you to have the tools and knowledge to find your rhythm. When you find your rhythm, it becomes infectious to others. In fact, you give others permission to be authentic when they see you confidently and unapologetically living out your purpose without fear or compromise. You will walk and operate in a stride of confidence that will signal to others, I am taking my rightful place in corporate America. Your pace and cadence of how you live will show others how to live and thrive. You will restore hope in others that they too can be exactly who the universe designed them to be.

Authentic Rhythm

Rhythm, by definition, is a strong, repeated pattern of movement or sound, principally according to duration and periodic stress, comprising all the elements (such as accent, beat, meter, and tempo) that relate to forward movement.

What is an Authentic Rhythm? Living your truth in a way that honors all your unique attributes, dimensions of difference, gender, culture, skills, and experiences without fear, allowing you to thrive at your peak performance in all you do.

Life in and of itself is a rhythm. We all have experienced different tempos, some fast and some slow. You may have even referred to this as life's ups and downs. I feel stuck, like I'm going in circles, or like I'm on a never-ending rollercoaster. These are only a few of life's rhythms I have identified as instruments toward understanding that any rhythm is appropriate as long as there is movement and improvement.

Give yourself grace, as finding one's authentic rhythm is a journey, a process, and not a destination. I have coined five fundamental principles that will guide you through the journey of *Finding Authentic Rhythm* to help you navigate the workplace and your personal life. These principles help you pivot when you get stuck and are offbeat or when life changes its beat and takes you off your rhythm. Let me introduce the principles that will help you find your rhythm and keep it.

5 Key Principles to Find Authentic Rhythm

1. Find Your Purpose and Your "Why"
2. Navigate the Unwritten Rules of Success in Corporate America
3. Become Strategic versus Busy
4. Standout on Purpose
5. Slay in Your Own Lane

Chapter by chapter, we will journey through a rhythmic tempo in hopes you catch the beat (pun intended!). At the end of each chapter, I will offer check-ins to make sure you are staying in tempo and finding your rhythm. The book is organized into five main tempos: Rhythmic-Less, Rhythmic Beat, Rhythmic Flow, Rhythmic Dance, and Rhythmic Sound.

Buckle up! Let's get ready to maximize your full potential, get your groove back, and dance!

TEMPO #1: RHYTHMIC-LESS

Chapter 1: What is Rhythmic Less?

"Vision is the true creative rhythm."
—Robert Delaunay

Have you ever heard the term "rhythmless"? Merriam-Webster's dictionary defines rhythmless as "devoid of rhythm." The simple working definition often refers to an individual that doesn't have any sequence to how they dance, move, or sing. It means you are all over the place; you lack tempo, pattern beat, and flow.

What does it mean to live Rhythmic-Less?

Rhythmic-Less is to live a life with no design or purposed direction. To just exist; one that has no understanding of their purpose or 'why' in life; to lack a consistent discipline in improving oneself and growth; to live with no flow; one that changes their goals and dreams daily with little to no direction and/or idea of their future.

In 1989, Janet Jackson released a song entitled *Rhythm Nation*. The song was a call to action and a blueprint for a better, more harmonious world. It was a vision of a world that offered rhythm, a better life, and purpose. The song began with these words:

With music by our side to break the color lines
Let's work together to improve our way of life
Join voices in protest against social injustice
A generation full of courage, come forth with me

People of the world today
Are we looking for a better way of life?
Sing!
We are a part of the Rhythm Nation.

The journey of authentic rhythm begins with, first and foremost, knowing who you are! You must do the work and start the self-discovery journey in defining your life. So let me introduce myself.

Who am I? I no longer define myself as Rhythmless. I am a devoted mother, loving daughter, wife, loyal friend, courageous corporate executive, motivational speaker, passionate career coach, and inspiring author. I have spent over twenty-five years designing human capital solutions that drive peak performance in corporate America. I've worked in both for-profit and nonprofit organizations. I have dedicated my career to making society better and advocating for women, people of color, and other marginalized and underrepresented groups. I am an advocate for social justice, racial equity, and fairness for all mankind.

I have been married to the love of my life, Tyron, for over twenty-eight years, and we have two young adult children, Taylor and Tyron Jr., and a grand dog, Ryder. I have four generations of women living in my family. I am a serial entrepreneur and an introvert who fakes extroversion masterfully. At my core, I am a woman who grew up as a little girl in Memphis, Tennessee who wanted to heal the world and help people.

I am an agent of change who desires to speak more love and joy into the hearts and minds of everyone I am blessed and honored to meet. People who know me best say I am the perfect articulation of my name, JOY.

I have worked in diversity, equity, and inclusion (DEI) for a large part of my career. I have served as the Chief DEI Officer for three Top Fortune 200 global companies under the leadership of five different CEOs. I have coached CEOs and executive leaders throughout my career on what it means to be a servant leader and how to lead more inclusively. I have led talent management functions and witnessed the good, bad, and ugly of organizational cultures. I have experience presenting to the Board of Directors and shareholders on human capital strategies. I've had a front-row seat to conversations that will remain private. I have had the opportunity to get "proximate" to the real feelings that exist in the halls of many organizations as it relates to race, gender identity, religion, sexual orientation, and many other dimensions of difference. I've also had the fortune of working with courageous leaders who have fought and advocated to advance and provide equity and fairness for all.

I am also a woman that allowed others' perceptions of me, along with my desire to be successful, change me early in my career. I lost my authenticity for years trying to fit into a culture called corporate America. I have been coached, mentored, and counseled on numerous things that challenged my authenticity—how to wear my hair, the color of my hair, what colors I should and shouldn't wear on my fingernails, etc. You would probably be surprised at what I had been taught and told to change.

Over time and over the years, the concept of proving myself stripped away my love for what I got up and did every morning. I no longer enjoyed going to work every day and that needed to change. I had to do the work to find myself and my authentic rhythm.

I fundamentally believe you can't understand where you are going if you don't know where you have been. Revisiting your past is an important first step in understanding if and when you lost your rhythm. A key life experience that compromises your authenticity can be traced back to when you first felt different. You can learn a lot from what happened and how you responded.

When Did I First Feel Different?

As a little girl growing up, my first introduction to being different centered around my skin color. Unfortunately, even today, skin color can sometimes serve as a criterion in determining how a person will be evaluated, treated, and judged. It is a sad reality that many face but we recognize and make the necessary adjustments to maintain our rhythm. In this country, because of deeply-entrenched racism, many still experience the ugliness of its impact. It cannot be overstated that if racism didn't exist, a discussion about varying skin hues would simply be a conversation of aesthetics. But that's not the case.

As early as I remember, children teased me because of my fair complexion. They made up hurtful and insensitive stories about how my skin became so light.

I remember it just like it was yesterday. It was my first day of kindergarten at Walker Elementary in Memphis, Tennessee. I could hardly sleep the night before as I was nervous and excited about my first day of school. I walked into the classroom, and a cute little boy came and pointed at me and said, "Oooh, you are White!"

I replied in a loud and affirmative tone, "No, I am not! I am Black."

He said, "No, you are not. Black people don't have green eyes and White skin."

I looked around the room and noticed many children laughing at his insidious comment. My eyes were glued to the door, longing for someone to walk in with similar physical characteristics so they would know I, too, was Black. I knew that in my family, I looked somewhat different than my cousins and the children in my neighborhood. They had gorgeous hues of beautiful brown skin. They had stunning black and brown eyes.

My eyes were another unique feature of discussion as they change color or appear to change colors. The colors range from grey/blue to green to hazel. Over the years, kids thought this attribute was spectacular and often waited to see what my eyes would look like on any given day. This characteristic further enhanced the teasing, and I was still referred to as a "White girl."

Sitting in the classroom on my first day, I pondered, *Why did he say that? What makes him think I am not Black? Will I be teased every day about my skin color?*

I wanted to go back home as I just wanted to fit in and make friends. What I thought would be a great first day turned out to be the opposite. I was confused. Why would people think I was not Black?

Valerie, who later became my childhood best friend, came over and said, "She is Black, her daddy is White, and that is why she looks like that. Duh, everybody knows that when Black people have green eyes, they have a White daddy. Ain't that true?" she asked of me.

I didn't know what to say or how to respond. If I shared that my dad was Black, they would continue to ask ignorant questions, further infuriating me. So, what did I do? I lied and said, "My daddy is White, so leave me alone!"

On the walk home, I thought long and hard about my lie. I felt horrible, but I was tired of people treating my mom like she wasn't my mother. Kids can say cruel things that can have lifelong impacts on one's image. Some of the experiences I had and the things kids said to me throughout the years are still hurtful today. They would say I was the result of a White man having an inappropriate relationship with my mom. I was ashamed and hurt by these ridiculous stories. So, how did I respond and deal with the pressure?

Unfortunately, I lied, and just like that, I lost my authentic rhythm in kindergarten. This would be a skill over time that I mastered for all the wrong reasons.

I've never shared with my mom how much it hurt as a child when people would see us together and immediately ask if she was my babysitter or nanny. Still, today, we've never talked about it. I am somewhat nervous as to how she will respond when reading this part of the book.

Ridiculously, my classmates assumed that because of her beautiful brown skin, there was no way she was my mother. Time and time again, this bothered me to my core. I was angry as I believed the ignorance of others hurt my mom, and it broke me too. I've never even shared with my mom that I lied about my father's race at such a young age. Little did I know, I was mastering a horrible skill in denying who I was to make others comfortable and to be accepted. Maybe

I did this because I didn't understand the concept of colorism.

Wow! The desire to be accepted and valued is powerful. It is a struggle that surpasses early childhood. Unfortunately, many adults never find their authentic rhythm, particularly for women, diverse, minority, and underrepresented groups in corporate America. Day in and day out, we mask our true selves for fear that we won't be good enough, safe enough, accepted enough, or loved enough to have a fair chance at success.

We have been coached or conditioned that for us to succeed in our careers, we must be the "model minority," the "submissive woman," the "safe Brown person," and the "unicorn minority." We were given "nice" advice that the more we align with the majority population, the greater our chances of success.

While I didn't lie anymore about my father's race, as I grew older, the damage remained and carried me through many years of my career. I learned how to give up, deny, and hide pieces and parts of myself to be successful and accepted. The sad reality was that I wasn't consciously aware of how pervasive this denial was in my life. I had become numb to my honest feelings of hurt. I worked so hard to please others that I forgot what pleased ME!

Fear happens to the best of us. For some, we have become conditioned to hide our true selves. We don't even recognize our authentic voice because it has been muted. We have been trained not to speak up and use our agent when it differs from others. Some of us have masked our voices for so long, we have forgotten how it sounds.

As a woman of color, I knew my skin was the first thing many saw when I entered a conference room. Unfortunately, some people are still uncomfortable and afraid of the Black race and people of color. This shows up in subtle and unsubtle ways that continue to rob us of our chances of success.

Early in my career, I remember meeting with my male boss. I was a Director then and grateful to have reached a level in my career that others desired and few attained that looked like me. We had our monthly one-on-one meeting. I was pitching an idea to change our leadership development programs to offer targeted solutions for women and people of color. I believed our recruiting and succession planning solutions did not address the challenges people of color were facing at our company.

At some point in the dialogue, he looked at me and said, "Joy, I am an inclusive leader. I don't think we have the *right* pipeline of talent inside the company to fill our representation gaps. We've been trying to improve our diversity numbers, but we don't have the skilled talent to put in these roles."

He continued by saying, "What do representation and race have to do with this? When I look at you, I don't see race!"

As I sat there, my emotions began to take flight. I immediately felt offended and disrespected. Our corporate leadership training had taught us repeatedly to assume good intent, but his statement was both hurtful and offensive, and I could not ignore its impact on me.

When he spoke the words, "I don't see race," I inherently heard, "You don't see me, and you are invalidating my race to make yourself comfortable."

I pondered as I knew I had a choice to make. This was my leader, the man in charge of influencing my career. I was early in my tenure at the organization. I had heard rumors about him as it related to being non-inclusive. I had even witnessed his shadow of leadership when people challenged or disagreed with him. Challenging him was problematic. Experience had shown me and others that if you challenged him, you would be labeled and deemed as difficult to work with. Ultimately, this would result in delayed or halted career progression.

My inner voice spoke to me.

Joy, you can be "safe" and choose "good intent," or you can be courageous and share how this comment made you feel.

My thoughts ranged from:

How dare he say some bull crap like this to me. How disrespectful. He should know better.

How would he like it if someone said those words to him? Joy, if you say something, you know you will not get promoted again, which will impact your career.

Wait, what if I were to help him feel his words' impact on something HE valued?

Would that work? I think that is the solution. Show him how it feels!

I sat back in my chair and remembered that courage comes with a cost. Challenging the mindset of others is not easy. Helping people to truly see bias in all its ugly forms is the work I was destined to do. It is my purpose, and I needed to own it and help him. Too often, we excuse inappropriate comments and destructive behaviors under the auspices of good intent. The work I've experienced in diversity, equity, and inclusion has taught me that we have over-anchored on this concept at the expense of never addressing the impact or the persons responsible for the effect. Those who continue to get hurt repeatedly are the marginalized, the underrepresented, and the underserved. They deserve better, and each of us has a role and responsibility to no longer weaponize people who are negatively impacted by telling them, "Just assume good intent."

Today, you will learn just how it feels to be unacknowledged.

I looked him squarely in the eyes and stated, "You know what, Martin, I understand your sentiment because when I see you, I don't see a father. I just see you."

Okay, I think I am in big trouble. His eyes appear as though they are about to pop out. His skin is turning red, and he looks pissed off!

Okay, Joy, you got this started, so now you must go all the way to show him. There is no turning back now.

He has repeatedly shared that I can be honest with him.

Girl, they all say that. You know it is not true. It's just nice words to say. Well, it is time to find out.

During our time together, I learned that he absolutely adored his daughters and often shared how proud he was to be a father. There were very few times we met in which he didn't have a story to tell about his children. Clearly, being a father was critical to him and something he valued. He was unapologetically clear that he loved faith and family. So, I knew my comment would strike a nerve for him, just as race did with me.

I said, "Martin, I understand your perspective because when I see you, I don't see a father. I just see a person, a human being."

I paused for a moment.

"By the look on your face, it appears as though you are offended."

He frantically said, "Well, yes, what do you mean you

don't see a father? I love my girls. Why would you say that?"

I said, "Exactly, and I love my skin and embrace all my Blackness. When you courageously said that you don't see race, it made me feel invisible. I know you might have been trying to say that race doesn't define how you see me. But the truth is, it would be virtually impossible for you to see me visually and not see the hue and color of my skin. Martin, I need you to see my race!

When you see race, you might recognize that my lived experiences may be different from yours. When you see my race, you see a remarkable history of resilience, perseverance, and fortitude. You see the diversity of thought and perspectives that can help offer solutions to people that look like me and others. When you see my race, you see a culture I love, and I would choose over and over again to be Black. When you see my race, you see a loving, caring, and often misunderstood culture. And it is *only* when you see my race that you truly see all of me.

It hurt me at the core when you said you don't see race. I am sure it hurt when I said I didn't see your parental status.

Martin, no one should have the right to deny seeing an important part of who a person is. It feels dishonoring to ignore and reduce any part of a human being."

He replied, "Wow, I felt that. I understand. No one has ever shown me how that *feels*. I thought I was doing the right thing by saying that I don't see race. Now I understand better, and I will NEVER say that again. Thank you for helping me to FEEL and learn."

I said, "It is only through the acknowledgment of seeing things that we are poised to address them. If you don't see the problem, how can you create change? I need you to see my race, I need you to see my gender, I need you to hear my accent, and I need you to respect all of who I am. When you truly see me, it means you are open to understanding me."

Just like that, in a moment, things changed for us.

He cowered in his chair, and we had the most vulnerable, sincere, and authentic conversation ever. We let the politically-correct walls down and had a vulnerable and raw conversation about race. We ended the meeting with a more open, honest, and trusting relationship. He asked me if I would coach him in his journey of being more self-aware of how he was either contributing to the solution or further advancing the challenges that minority populations were experiencing.

> **Teaching Point:** Never challenge leadership in a group setting on their growth areas. You are better suited to reach them if you have a one-to-one dialogue in a safe environment that honors their position but also speaks truth to power.

Rhythm Check: ♪ 🥁

Understanding one's authentic nature requires revisiting your life to find the moment or event that caused you to change or give up a little piece of who you were. This work is not easy, but necessary to understand *who* you are. How can you discover authenticity without revisiting your beginning—the core of who you are?

1. When reading this section, what story did you remember from your past?
2. What was the first time you felt different? How did you respond and why?
3. How old were you? And what was going on in your life at the time?
4. What made you deny or change something about yourself?
5. When did you lose your authentic rhythm?

Chapter 2: Purpose

*"Music and rhythm find their way into the
secret places of the soul."*
—Plato

Each of us in life is on a journey to find our purpose. Whether in our careers, family, finances, health, relationships, or within ourselves, we long for fulfillment and happiness that might sometimes seem impossible to define. We search over and over again, looking for our life's mission or purpose.

We long to understand our unique talent or value proposition. For many, this is a quest that seems unattainable. I have great news! You can find your purpose if you are willing to be honest with yourself, put in the time, work, and effort to understand the most arduous question in life- what is my purpose?

Only about a quarter of Americans report having a clear sense of purpose and understanding of what makes their lives meaningful. Research increasingly suggests that purpose is essential for a meaningful—and healthy—life. When coaching women, one of the first questions I ask is *What is your purpose?*

Time and time again, women share that they do not know their purpose. They seek coaching, mentoring, and often counseling to help them discover and find the answer to life's most arduous question. Throughout my journey, I, too, struggled to answer this question. I didn't know my purpose.

I remember looking in the mirror one day, and I didn't recognize Joy. I was the version in the mirror that my parents *taught* me to be. I was the version that my husband *wanted* me to be. And I was the person my church *told* me to be and the person my job *required* of me. I never took the time to think about who I wanted to be.

I WAS EXHAUSTED…and LOST!

Many women report feelings very similar to my experience. They struggle with happiness and fulfillment. They are defined by their relationship or parental status, and the pressure can be daunting. They are repeatedly asked:

Are you married?

When are you getting married?

Are you dating? If not, why aren't you?

Do you have children? If not, what are you waiting on?

How many children do you want?

These questions come with a high degree of judgment based on the answer. Many women leave these conversations feeling as though they are failing. I submit to you that it's because you haven't figured out your purpose. Women are so much more than their careers, relationships, and parental status. Let's rewrite this norm, regain your power, and find your purpose!

Finding your purpose is more than a cliché or an exercise to fulfill your dreams. It's a tool for a better, happier, and healthier life. The wonderful news is that you don't have to choose between happiness and success. You can have them both. A 2016 study published in the *Journal of Research and Personality* found that individuals who feel a sense of purpose make more money than those who feel their work lacks meaning. You can have a happy life and be successful in your career if you are willing to engage in a process that allows you to better understand your wants, needs, strengths, and opportunities.

"Having a purpose in your life is also linked to many positive health outcomes, including better sleep, fewer strokes and heart attacks, and a lower risk of dementia, disability, and premature death.

Knowing your purpose is like writing the title of your life's book.

What is the title of the life you were designed to live?

Take a moment to reflect. What should be the title of your life's book if you were living in your purpose?

In this gift called life, we are a book that people read every day. Whether we want them to or not, we are telling a story to the world, and they are reading. How you present yourself to others and how people experience you are chapters to your living novel. It's your bestseller. How would you rewrite the next chapter if you were intentionally living in your purpose?

If you do not know your purpose, your life's beat and rhythm are off!

FINDING YOUR PURPOSE

There are four primary steps to finding your purpose. Let's get started. The rhythm of your life is first and foremost dependent upon knowing your purpose. You cannot live in authenticity without knowing why you exist and what you can contribute to this gift called life. Finding your purpose requires four key steps:

1. Self-Assessment
2. Assessment by Others
3. Get Visual
4. Reflect and Create the Plan

Step 1: Self-Assessment

Finding your purpose is one of life's most exciting and scariest goals. We often look for answers in others, but in most cases, the answers begin with us. You are worth investing in.

Think of yourself as a brand. One year from today, how do you want your life to look? What goals do you want to have accomplished? What new beginnings and memories do you want to create? These are the type of questions you should begin to ask yourself.

Now, take the time and answer the following questions below truthfully, and don't be afraid to dream BIG! This may require intentional time, so don't rush the process. The greatest disappointment in life is not failure, it's not trying! You owe it to yourself to spend the diligent time to understand YOU!

If your answers don't scare you or make you uncomfortable, maybe you aren't being honest. Chapters two and three of this book will require the most self-discovery and reflection. Be patient and trust the process. It is important that you commit to this journey in the next several pages.

10 critical questions that will change your life

1. What are you good at?
2. What are you passionate about?
3. If you could design the perfect life, how would it look?
4. If money were no object, what would be your dream job?

5. What skills come easy for you?
6. What activities make you happy and give you energy?
7. What are you doing when you lose track of time because you are having so much fun?
8. What impact do you want to make in the world?
9. What is your creative talent?
10. If you could write a billboard title for your dream life, what would it be?

Step 2: Assessment by Others

It is crucial to understand how others see and experience you. We are often the most demanding critics of ourselves. We live in fear and often miss the key messages and insights from others that we fundamentally need to hear, know, and understand.

Whatever your purpose is in life, I promise you that you have heard it repeatedly, but maybe you lack the confidence and willpower to activate it. Or you don't believe it.

Find 5 people that know you well. Choose people you trust to be unapologetically honest with you.

Simply ask them these three questions:
1. What three words would you use to describe me if I was a brand?
2. If I was to start a business, what would be the industry, and what would I be doing?

3. What is my most outstanding skill or talent?

Please make sure to listen without judgment. This is an opportunity to understand what others see and value in you.

Write down their answers.

Step 3: Get Visual

A vision board is one key action you should put on your to-do list and do it quickly. Vision boards have been fundamental in helping me achieve success as a mom, wife, friend, leader, author, and career-driven woman.

What is a vision board?

Simply put, a vision board is about creating your life's future through imagery. It is a visual articulation of what is most important to you. What if I told you that a vision board could be one of the most potent tools and activities you could engage in this year to reach many of your aspirations?

Getting visual allows you to imagine a future that doesn't currently exist.

Here are some of the benefits of a vision board and why it's different:

- *Vision boards allow you to spend reflective time with yourself to better understand yourself.*
- *A vision board acknowledges and incorporates your*

feelings!

- *A vision board gives you permission to see yourself and acknowledge your desires.*
- *A vision board is a mental exercise.*
- *A vision board helps to ground you.*
- *A vision board helps others see YOU.*

Step 4: Reflect and Create the Plan

Throughout my life, reflecting has been one of the most soul-healing methods to help me find my purpose. It helped me better understand who I am and acknowledge my failures, disappointments, and fears, but also my accomplishments, triumphs, and successes.

The more I reflected, the better I became at the art of reflection, and so will you. Start by setting aside seven minutes daily to reflect and converse with yourself. Concentrate on what brings you energy, how you want to spend the day, and what helps you feel fulfilled.

At the end of each week, ask yourself the following:

- What are the common themes?
- What surprised you the most and why?
- What did you learn about yourself that you didn't know?
- What provided confirmation and validation?
- What made you uncomfortable? Why?

Review what you learned from your self-assessment and feedback from others. Consolidate the feedback and insights from Steps 1-3. You should now see themes and commonalities.

Based on everything you have learned, answer the question: What is my purpose or unique talent in life?

_____

_____

_____

Trust me, you know the answer based on the work. Now write an affirmation statement and OWN IT!

Affirmation Statement: (ex., I commit to writing 3+ hours per week to finish my novel.)

After I completed steps 1-3, my purpose became crystal clear. My life's purpose is to SPEAK JOY. Your life's purpose can be as simple as two words. Learning your purpose provides clarity and liberty in everything you do. It should guide your decisions and actions going forward in every aspect of your life.

Rhythm Check: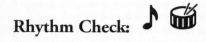

Understanding your purpose is a crucial step in finding your authentic rhythm. You won't know your beat or tempo if you don't know the music of your life.

1. Did you find the exercise of getting clear on your life's purpose easy or difficult? Why or why not?
2. How comfortable are you in sharing with purpose with others?
3. Commit to share this purpose with others! It will help you to stay grounded and affirm your purpose. Remember to only share this with people who have demonstrated a positive mindset. Also, share your purpose with your mentor.
4. What did you learn about yourself from others that made you curious to learn more?
5. Write your purpose in your organizer, planner, or anywhere that allows you to stay focused and revisit it often.

Chapter 3: Your "Why"

"Life has its rhythm, and we have ours. They're designed to coexist in harmony so that when we do what is ours to do and otherwise let life be, we garner acceptance and serenity."
—Victoria Moran

YOUR WHY

Now that you have figured out your purpose and affirmed it, let's seek to understand your "why." Why is it important to understand your *why?* Your *why* is a statement describing why you do the work you do and why you live your life the way you do. It provides clarity and helps you prioritize where you spend your time and talents. It can also help you understand the line of business you engage in or the type of work you should be doing.

Often, people feel stuck in careers because they are busy

doing what others choose for them versus their own career choices. Some are even lost on what they want or the direction their life should take. It is often due to their early dreams, desires, and preferences being dismissed, marginalized, and judged by others. Judgment can be a career and a dream killer!

If you are lost, most likely your dreams have been mentally beaten down so much or not believed in that you have no idea what you want to do. You have lost your way. You lack direction and support. No one believes in your dreams, so you stopped dreaming!

Think of your *why* as:
- Your **life compass:** It tells you which direction to go.
- Your **reason:** It gives your life's work purpose.
- Your **guiding light:** It pushes you past your struggles and fears.
- Your **mission:** It connects you to something bigger than you.
- Your **values:** It holds a deep meaning to something important.
- Your **career story:** It's why you do what you do.
- Your **inspiration:** It's how you motivate yourself and others.
- Your **hope:** It helps you to stay focused on the bigger picture.
- Your **manifesto:** It gives you pride.

Finding your *why* requires reimaging your life. It is at the foundation of getting unstuck in your career. It requires three key steps:

1. **Dream:** start by picturing your ideal workday. Don't listen to the noise that is trying to stop your rhythm. Picture it and own it. Reject the need to lose courage in answering these questions. As you envision your ideal workday:

    o Where are you?

    o What are you doing?

    o What is the environment like?

    o Are you primarily working with objects or people?

    o How are you contributing to the work?

    o What is your role?

    o What makes this day ideal?

2. **Reflect:** think of when you have been the most productive.

    o What were you doing?

    o Why were you productive?

    o Were you productive due to skill, passion, or both, and why?

3. **Acknowledge:** acknowledge what is important to you.

    o What do you value?

    o What matters to you?

    o What or who gets you out of bed to do what you do?

Finding your *why* elevates your purpose. It provides the missing ingredient to fulfilling your purpose. People might know their purpose and calling in life, but they are unmotivated to activate it. When you understand your values and why you do what you do, your purpose will become more significant than you, and then it will have meaning. Your *why* allows your purpose to be manifested.

A *why* is different for everyone. It can be as simple as a loved one or a goal, or it can be tied to a mission, life calling, destination, or legacy. Whatever the reason, your *why* is critical to achieving the life and career you so desperately deserve and desire.

HOW I DISCOVERED MY WHY

When I was a young girl, my uncle came back from the military very different from how he left. We didn't truly understand why he was different. There were so many opinions and judgments. We tried to pray it out, anoint it out. You name it—we tried it. But none of it worked.

The experience profoundly impacted me. It also caused and designed my destiny. At that young age, I knew I wanted to understand mental health and mental well-being so I could advocate for other families who were going through what my family went through and help them navigate the journey differently.

The experience with my uncle steered my career direction and aspirations. It is why I started my career in mental health.

But keep in mind, your *why* is not static. It evolves. Although mental health was my beginning, I was open to God's destinations and later in life, my *why* evolved even more.

My older sister and I were very close. Shauntel (we called her Shaun) and I never wanted to be apart. Either I was at her house, or she was at mine. Although we were opposites in many areas, our personalities complemented one another. She was my alter ego. While Shaun was soft-spoken and somewhat shy (if she didn't know you), I was outspoken and did the talking for both of us. I had a mild temperament, and it took a lot to get me upset, while Shaun was a force to be reckoned with if she got angry. All in all, we were each other's protectors.

We had our first and only fight when we were about twelve years of age. I remember her lying in bed. She looked at me and said, "Mom said we should never go to bed angry with one other. Please talk to me. I said I was sorry."

I relented and said, "Okay."

Shaun said, "I don't know what I would do if you weren't in my life. When we get older, I hope I never have to bury you. I would be a mess. I think I would be laid on the floor crying at the funeral."

"Shaun, let's not talk about this. That's sad. I hope I never have to bury you, either. Okay, I forgive you. Now stop being so melodramatic, and let's go to sleep!"

In 2013, my sister became ill and was later diagnosed with the big "C." Months later, she had an outpatient procedure that should have been simple and non-life threatening. She came home and told me she should feel a small degree of pain for a couple of days but should heal and return to regular duties in less than a week. A few hours after getting settled at home, I called to check on her. She shared that she was in pain beyond what she expected. I strongly encouraged her to call the doctor and share that she was hurting badly.

She complied, called me back, and said, "They said the pain is normal. Take a pain pill, and I should be remarkably better by tomorrow morning."

"Shaun, are you sure? Don't you think you should go to the hospital if you're hurting that bad?" I asked.

"Well, if I don't feel better in a couple of hours, I'll call them back. I promise." She assured me.

Hours later, she called the doctor and was told the pain was normal and to take more pain pills. I tried to call her, but unfortunately, my sister didn't answer. The following day, I called repeatedly. No answer. Something in my gut didn't feel right. I knew something was wrong. I called my brother-in-law, who was at work. He told me he thought my sister was asleep due to all the medicines she had taken and not to worry. I was still not satisfied because I needed to hear my sister's voice. It was not like her to ignore my calls. I then called my niece, her adult daughter, and told her to check on her mom.

My niece called and said my sister was nonresponsive and

that she was calling 911. By the time my sister arrived at the hospital, she was septic. She was on life support for several days. The healthcare system failed her, and they failed my family. Her pain was real, and it was an indication that something had gone wrong with the procedure. I later learned that she called repeatedly to get help, only to be told her pain was normal. How many times have women of color died because healthcare practitioners ignored their pain?

Racial and ethnic disparities in pain treatment are not intentional misdeeds. Healthcare providers do not intentionally decide that some groups deserve pain relief while others should suffer. Instead, inequities are the product of complex influences, including implicit biases that care providers don't even know they have. Moreover, false ideas about women and especially women of color's pain can lead to treatment disparities. I share this story in hopes that it will help others advocate more strongly for women's health. I also share this to help you understand how life events can impact our rhythm and impact our *why*.

Over the following weeks, I struggled with grief. I was depressed and couldn't sleep. I didn't want to leave Memphis, where my sisters, parents, and family lived. And I didn't want to return to work.

I learned about an opportunity in an area closer to Memphis, with a pharmaceutical company with a successful portfolio in oncology. My mentor advised that this would allow me to do the work in my sister's name. It would make my *why* clear. In some small way, I would have a chance to make a difference, to make life better for people around the world. So healthcare is the space I want to contribute my life's best work, and my sister is absolutely my *why*.

Today, I help build strategies to enhance outcomes for women and underserved people. My career is directly tied to my purpose and divine assignment in life. Every opportunity I have, I want to help others advocate for women and women of color in the healthcare system in a way that lives are saved. I am living out my purpose and my *why*.

Rhythm Check: ♪ 🥁

Let's recap the three steps to understanding your *why*.

1. Dream: Describe a perfect day at work. What makes it ideal?
2. Reflect: When was the last time you felt productive? What were you doing? Why did you feel productive?
3. Acknowledge: What matters to you? What or who gets you out of bed to do what you do?

TEMPO #2:
RHYTHMIC-BEAT

Chapter 4: Off-Beat!

"Where I come from, we say that rhythm is the soul of life because the whole universe revolves around rhythm, and when we get out of rhythm, that's when we get into trouble."
—Babatunde Olatunji

Rhythmic beat in music is characterized by a repeating sequence of stressed and unstressed beats (often called "strong" and "weak") and divided into bars organized by time signature and tempo indications.

Dr. Joe Dispenza says that in our late twenties to early thirties, we live in two ways: *survival* or *expansion*. Have you ever felt like you were just surviving or going through the motions? Have you ever felt disconnected, offbeat, or out of sync? There was a season when I felt emotionally and culturally disconnected at work and in the city where I lived. I felt the beat of my life was off, out of sync, and off pace. I lacked a genuine connection with my coworkers. There were many days I felt out of place. I desired authentic relationships at work and desperately wanted to feel like I belonged. I guess you could say my rhythmic beat was off!

Let's start with the word *culture* and the root word *cult*. Culture can be defined by a group's shared beliefs, values, and characteristics. Culture can be connected to gender, race, religion, geography, age, ethnicity, etc. Culture is experienced as your way of life. It's your comfort zone, your norm. It's your place of safety. It's your place of love. And it's your place of connections.

In workplace cultures, this is often referred to as cultural fit. Meaning, do you "fit in" to how things are done at your organization. Are you agile enough to assimilate to the norms and practices of the company? Will you be intuitive in replicating the unwritten rules of the culture? Or will you try to change things and disrupt how things are done?

Cultural fit, in some cases, can work in opposition to diversity and inclusion. I have seen this used as a way to deny women and minority populations opportunities to advance in their careers. It is essential to use cultural fit in the proper context, which is ensuring the talent aligns with the values and leadership principles of the organization.

People are cultural creatures. The first cultural connections are typically created within the family, which shape how we view ourselves and what we value. Your family and cultural upbringing impact how you see mental health and well-being, including how you are taught to handle challenges and challenging circumstances, how you talk about them, with whom you share them, and how you seek support.

Your cultural upbringing may also influence how you unwind, care for yourself, and handle conflict. Maintaining a connection to your "home culture" can be challenging when one encounters and engages with many different cultures.

We are surrounded by culture, which gives us the means to communicate and connect. Although culture is connected to people and a shared identity, it is also connected to geographical areas. Many people who live abroad may experience cultural disconnection—living in a neighborhood where some facets of your culture are disapproved of, such as your identity, values, or sexual orientation, can be detrimental to your welfare. Conflict over your cultural identity may arise if you live in a place where the majority culture is different from your own or shows little tolerance for it.

You may start to wonder who you are and if you belong. At times you may feel cut off from your cultural roots. You could feel alone and lost because of this. Connecting with culture can positively impact your sense of identification and belonging, which can improve your mental health and general welfare.

I was born and raised in Memphis, Tennessee. Three of my core and most important values are faith, family, and friends. In May of 2007, my husband came home and shared that he wanted to have a meaningful discussion. He excitedly shared that he was in the final round of an interview for a job that would require relocation to the Midwest. We'd had this type of conversation many times before but based on the look in his eyes and the overwhelmingly excited tone in his voice, I knew this time, the conversation would be different. I needed to listen differently and with an open mind. In the past, I wasn't open to having a meaningful conversation about relocation. I would shut down the conversation immediately.

"Babe, where is this company located?" I asked.
"Cedar Rapids, Iowa."
"Cedar Rapids! I've never even heard of Cedar Rapids. Why would we want to go to Iowa, of all places? Are there any people that look like me there?"

I began to do my research, and at that time in the small rural town of Cedar Rapids, African Americans accounted for one to two percent of the population. I remember praying and asking, *"Lord, please help me figure this out because my family and faith are very much connected to Memphis. All my support systems—my mother, my siblings, my parents, and my husband's family—are in Memphis. I have two young children, and I need to be strong for them, but I don't want to go. I think this will be a good move for my husband's career but not for me."*

This would be a significant change in all our lives, and I was emotionally terrified. I tried my best to hide my real feelings. I am a woman of faith, and all critical decisions in my life are guided by trusting in God to help reveal the path and journey I should take. In previous times when I shared that Tyron had gotten a job offer out of town, my mother and grandmother were the first to say, "You guys don't need to move. Tyron is doing well here and has a great job. The children are small, and it would be too much change for a dual-career family." I felt the same way, so their input was music to my ears.

But there was something strange and different this time. When I shared with my mother and grandmother the opportunity in Cedar Rapids, they acknowledged it as a great opportunity for the family. I was in shock! Surprisingly, they were both supportive.

I have the utmost respect for the women in my family. They are strong, resilient, faithful, kind, loving, and most of all, spiritual prayer warriors. I trust their advice and wisdom explicitly, but this time my faith and trust waivered.

So, I decided to call the "big gun," my great-grandmother, who is the matriarch of our family. I talked to her about the decision, and she, too, was supportive!

What in the world is going on? Why do they think this is a good thing? On the inside, I was breaking, and they didn't even see it. I DO NOT WANT TO MOVE TO IOWA!

I then thought, *Let me give this one more try. I am going to call my pastor. I know he will seek God's advice and provide me with another answer.* I just knew I would get a different response from him. Well, to my surprise, he was also supportive of the move. I will never forget the words he shared with me that day. It blessed me, and I hope it blesses you.

Pastor: This is God's will. It might not look or feel like it, but know that God has created this opportunity to be a blessing for you and your family.

Me: But I don't want to leave. All my family is here.

Pastor: Your family is wherever you, your husband, and your children are. You can accomplish anything as long as you and he are on one accord and united. Your blessing will come in you exercising your faith.

Me: I worry about my children and my relationships with the family.

Pastor: You don't lose anything built and grounded in love. Sometimes, you have to leave to grow. Growth is not easy. It's hard but necessary to fulfill the purpose that lies in you. I promise you that you will look back one day and understand why this was an essential step in your journey. There is a light in you that needs to shine in ways that this move will allow and manifest. It will get tough. It will get hard but trust the process. You have been conditioned for this, and you are ready!

I submitted to the decision. We took a site visit to Cedar Rapids, and a month later, I was also offered a job in human resources to help create a curriculum in diversity and inclusion. I was elated to take on the role. It was an area of passion and also one in which I had experience.

Key Teaching Point: you will later see how this move catapulted my career. Success is not easy. It is a journey that requires conditioning and growth. Don't be afraid to step out and grow!

Months later, my family relocated and started our new journey. As I began working at a new company, one key thing was missing: genuine connections with other women. Day in and day out, I would attend meetings in hope and sheer desperation, longing to see someone that looked like me. Can you imagine going months and months feeling alone, isolated, and different? Most days were very uncomfortable. I faked it and tried to show everyone that I was okay, but I wasn't. I sought solace in my work and my family. I poured every ounce of my energy into my job and the children. They were my safe place, my haven.

The music and the tempo in my life were different. The beat wasn't my norm, and I tried my best to find the beat or any beat that would fill the gaps I was missing. In essence, you can describe this as a season of cultural disconnection in the tempo of my life.

You might wonder what cultural disconnection has to do with finding authentic rhythm. Our shared culture unites us. It crosses all lines. Culture is passed down through family, language, and customs. Since everyone's definition of culture is unique, there are countless ways to define it.

There are four critical aspects of being culturally disconnected. Cultural connections and disconnections can alter and affect how you view and experience the world. They can derail your career and your ability to feel fulfilled.

Four Aspects of Being Culturally Disconnected

1. Feeling Uniquely Different, in a Nonvalue Added Way
2. Feeling Left Out
3. Feeling Judged
4. Feeling Like You Need to Change to be Accepted

1. Feeling Different

Social isolation in the workplace can erode your ability to feel like you belong. As human beings, we look for connections to feel valued and respected. Many enter workplace environments seeking relationships to enhance their ability to get work done.

On any given day, most likely, you experience more time with colleagues than you do with family and friends. So, it is critically important to feel connected to those with whom you work. The more you see commonalities between yourself and others in the workplace, the more likely you feel part of the team or organization. Quite the opposite, when you feel different and lack connections, it is harder to feel welcomed and valued.

Individuals who come to work every day and feel as if they don't belong expend a great deal of energy trying to be accepted, questioning why they aren't fitting in and what they can do to change. I felt uniquely different walking in the hallways every day at work. I was born and raised in the South but now lived in the Midwest, and my coworkers felt very comfortable pointing out my cultural differences.

I have a Southern accent, and people would often inquire where I was from. Until then, I had never felt uncomfortable with my accent. For the first time in my life, I recognized that many people place undue value on accents. They judge your level of intellect based on how you speak versus your ability to communicate effectively.

One day, I arrived early for a meeting. While sitting and waiting for others to come, a new person entered the room whom I had not met before. She looked me up and down and said, "Hi, I don't think we've met before. I am Karen."

"Hi Karen, I am Joy. It's very nice to meet you."

"I haven't seen you around. How long have you been with the company?"

"Social prejudice crosses the threshold of the workplace—preventing employers from creating inclusive cultures that allow *all* employees to do their best work."
—Coqual

"I've been here a few months."

"Where are you from? Based on your accent, I would assume you aren't from here. I am trying to determine where your accent is from. Let me guess."

By this time, other people began to join us in the conference room and listen to our conversation.

I am so tired of people asking me where I am from. Why does it really matter? Why is she asking me about my accent? I hope she is not trying to be disrespectful. Well, let's test this theory.

So, I replied, "I am doing the same thing. I am trying to figure out where you are from. I, too, detect an accent. Let me guess as well."

Her entire countenance changed, and the room became awkwardly quiet. All eyes began to focus on the two of us. She no longer looked happy. She looked pissed!

"What do you mean you heard an accent? I don't have an accent."

"Well, everyone has an accent, including you. Just as my tone and cadence of speech are different from yours. Your speech is different from mine. An accent is merely a distinction in how we pronounce words."

Sarcastically she replied, "Well, maybe you have a point. I just never thought I had an accent. I thought I talked *normal.*"

Did she just say "normal?" Wait...maybe I heard her wrong.

"So, are you saying my accent is not normal because it is different?"

Just then, another colleague spoke up and said, "I think what Karen is trying to say is that she didn't believe people from the Midwest were considered to have an accent. Karen, it's probably best if you don't point things out like this to people as it might make them feel uncomfortable. Okay, let's get the meeting started."

Wow, what a way to pivot but also address the elephant in the room.

In my mind, I am singing Beyonce's lyrics:
"And I don't feel bad about it
It's precisely what you get
Stop interrupting my grinding
I ain't thinking 'bout you

Sorry, I ain't sorry"

> **Teaching point:** It is not okay to highlight the differences of others in a way in which you make them feel as if their difference is wrong or inferior to you.

I don't believe Karen meant to call out my accent in an

honoring way. She was trying to point out a difference that she equated to social class and intellect. She was trying to highlight an area she thought would devalue me, and she got a taste of her own medicine! As my mom once told me, "You have to teach people how to treat you."

Unfortunately, accent is an area in which many biased associations are made. For instance, many people from the United States love to hear a British accent. Quite the opposite, if your accent is connected to Alabama or Mississippi, some might consider you less than, ignorant, unintelligent, and incapable of speaking correct grammar and English. I can't count the number of times people would say, "Oh, where are you from? I think I hear a little bit of a southern drawl."

Other times, I would get the opposite feedback. "Joy you are so articulate. You speak so well." These comments were never said in a way in which I felt valued or respected for growing up in the South. Quite the opposite, these comments made me feel inferior and less than. I began to hate my accent. I became nervous and self-conscious about how I spoke and enunciated my words for the first time in my life. I worked to get rid of my southern accent.

Many minorities come to work every day and try their hardest to speak in an accent that others deem more appropriate or intelligent while denying who they are and where they were born. I made sure I changed my tone and accent the best I could in the work setting. I even changed the pace in which I spoke to a slower pace because, in the South, we talk fast. While this started as a conscious effort to change and improve over time, I wasn't aware that I had two completely different voices and tones. My family and children often made me acutely aware of my "work" voice and my "home" voice. I've often wondered, how many of my colleagues have a "work" voice and a "home" voice.

Even the part of the world that I was raised in came with judgment. These differences weren't limited to speech and accent. Intellect was also linked to geography. A senior leader once told me to stop sharing that I was from Memphis, Tennessee. I should drop Memphis and only say Tennessee. Apparently, Memphis equated to the deep South culture, while other parts of Tennessee, such as Knoxville and Chattanooga, were considered a little more culturally appropriate and less threatening.

As it relates to accent:

- Always proceed with caution when thinking about highlighting a person's accent. In many cases, it is not received positively or considered a respectful question.
- Ask yourself, why is highlighting a person's accent important? What do you hope to gain from the acknowledgment? If you are interested in learning about their culture or origin, ask that instead!
- Never make fun of or mimic a person's accent.
- Never associate or equate intellect with a person's accent. This impacts one's ability to thrive inside an organization.

- Before you highlight a difference of another person, stop and ask, how might this make them feel?

2. Feeling Left Out

Workplace exclusion is a business issue. It impacts every part of the organization from the personal experience of the individual to performance, outcomes, and financial metrics. When people feel included, organizations benefit from getting the best out of them. They thrive! They feel safe to bring their best work and talents to the workplace. They experience inclusion at its best which is feeling welcomed, valued, respected, and heard. When performance increases, the business grows and excels.

Workplace inclusion also allows for innovation. When people feel included and valued, they feel safe to share their ideas and creative thoughts. They feel as though they are part of something bigger. Quite the opposite, social exclusion in a work environment can be septic to the individual, team dynamics, and performance, which negatively impacts the business. There is a financial cost and impact when organizations lose great talent. People who feel left out and excluded are more likely to quit. It is expensive and it disrupts the flow of performance on a team. It also can be toxic to the mental well-being of talent. When you continually feel excluded and left out, it robs you of your inner peace and confidence. Over time, it can cause you to question your self-worth and value.

I felt culturally disconnected and left out for a significant period in my career. I remember one day in particular. I was sitting in my office looking out the window at the mounds of snow. One of my peers started to walk down the hallway that connected all our offices. I could hear her stopping by everyone's office one-by-one, asking if they wanted to go out after work for drinks. This was a common practice of many of my colleagues. While I had never been invited or asked, something struck me differently while hearing this occur. I was anxiously anticipating that this would be the day. This would be the day I would get invited. There was no way in the world she would publicly announce this invitation to everyone and not include me. My presence alone would force her to invite me, or so I thought. I had been waiting on the invitation. My feelings had been hurt many times because I genuinely wanted to make friends and have deeper connections with my peers.

When she got to my door, she kept going and went to the next door and proceeded to invite everyone else. She literally looked at me and kept walking. I was stunned, hurt, and angry. I couldn't understand why I was not invited and left out.

In my first ninety days of joining the company, I had been told that the Midwest was its own culture. And that the Midwest culture was one in which people would be friendly but not always inclusive. In the Midwest, they had long, deep relationships that could be traced back to childhood. Their networks were hard to enter and even harder for those who were different.

I sat in my office and pondered the reality that I was a

long way from home, family, friends, and support. My children attended a Lutheran school, and we were the only Black family. When she walked past my office and didn't invite me, I thought I had made a horrible decision leaving my hometown and coming to Iowa for a career. I often pondered: What are my children experiencing, and how will this shape their authentic rhythm?

My Rhythmic Beat was off. I call it the "lonely is an only" syndrome. You're the only woman or person on your team who looks like you. Or the only person with your beliefs and values. It can be a very lonely place when you feel as if you don't have friends or authentic connections. And let's be clear. No one wants to be denied friendships because it's not accessible to them. Quite the opposite, you want to be able to say, I don't have any friends because I don't want friends. No one wants to feel like they don't have connections and friends because people deny them the opportunity to enter those relationships.

3. Feeling Judged

We all have moments in which we fear being judged by those we work with. We worry about their impressions of us and how that might impact our job or career mobility. We wonder what is said about us when we are not in the room. We fear being good enough, ready enough, and liked enough to be accepted. We believe the sales pitch that we are hired for our unique skills and abilities yet, the reality of many is quite the opposite. We quickly learn we must change because the real version of who we are is counter-cultural.

Feeling judged is a powerful derailer and confidence disrupter. It robs us of our authentic genius. It takes us out of our natural groove and disrupts our life beat. It takes you out of your authentic rhythm. It is weight to prove yourself worthy. You were raised and taught by your parents or loved ones that you are worthy but, in the work setting, many feel quite the opposite. Every action, every word, every decision, every statement, and every movement feels judged.

If you allow it, it will rob you of your peace and authentic nature. You might find yourself changing to be accepted and those changes might not be growth. You are not alone! I too felt judged and so do many others.

When you feel culturally disconnected, you have experiences, whether explicit or implicit, in which people make you feel wrong for being who you are. You've had experiences in which being who you uniquely are felt like a weight and a curse. You feel like it's of a lesser value or not culturally recognized with the same degree of respect and honor as others around you.

I felt judged on several things, but mostly I felt judged at the intersection of gender and race. For example, on Fridays, if they had fried food, someone would come to my door and say, "Hey, they have fried chicken. I know you like fried chicken." And let me be clear. I love fried chicken, but I didn't need them to tell me I love fried chicken. They never came by to share other food options.

"The emotional effects of ostracism are very real and can be severe. Loneliness, anger, shame — these all take a toll on a person."
—Bravely

I have also often been referred to or called "gal." I have been asked to go and get coffee for the men more times than I can count. But I have never been invited to play golf or attend after-work events with the men. This impacts our career opportunities because we lack access to deep relationships that occur in private settings.

I have also dealt with racism. The hate and insidiousness of feeling judged for my race escalated to a point in which the police once got involved. One evening on the ride home from work, as we entered our neighborhood, I saw that someone had spray painted on our neighborhood sign, "No n--gers allowed!" Several days later, they egged our home and cars.

My children were home alone when they egged our house. On another occasion, a friend's car was vandalized, and their car tires were slashed. The police were called, and they deemed it a hate crime based on the sequence of events.

> "According to researchers, the need to belong "is so basic to human behavior that the first premise of virtually every theory of social or cultural behavior could be that people have a pervasive drive to form and maintain at least a minimum quantity of lasting, positive, and significant interpersonal relationships."
>
> Marie Forleo

Many days I wanted to leave, pack up my home, and tell my husband, "You know what, I'm good. We're going back." But then, there was a sense of fight and resilience in me. I called home and shared with my mom that I struggled with having my children coming and going from school given what was happening in our neighborhood. I worried about their safety. My mom said sternly, "Let me tell you something. You went to Cedar Rapids on your own terms and will leave on your own terms. You don't let anybody run you off. Leave when you are ready. If they run you off, they win. Stay and finish what you went there to accomplish. Move to a new neighborhood but don't leave the city unless it is on YOUR terms. The problem is you have the wrong strategy in place. You're trying to fit in instead of blending in. You are changing and as your mom, I know it's not you. And it's not worth it."

4. Feeling Like You Need to Change to be Accepted

Finding your authentic rhythm and voice takes a lot of energy and courage, especially for women. Women take great pains to develop their voices, and my journey was no exception. I spent countless hours trying to come up with the right tone, the perfect facial expressions (smile), and the ideal posture, and it all became too much.

I had changed. If I went to work events, I didn't drink sweet tea, because that was a Southern drink. *And I LOVE sweet tea.* In an effort to lose my Southern accent, I would not talk a lot in open meetings. I didn't have many people who looked like me at work. Surprisingly a few shared that they were fine with having a relationship with me in private but not in public. It is not uncommon for minorities to feel unsafe connecting with other minorities publicity in the workplace.

Women are often the minority at senior tables in corporate America, especially in STEM fields. They are often overlooked and feel unheard. They struggle to feel respected to the same degree as their male counterparts. They fear they will be denied career opportunities due to their parental status. They overwork to prove they too can be the superwomen in their homes while trying to balance their career. This struggle comes at a cost, and many feel lost.

Rhythmic check: I was losing myself. Now from a career standpoint, everything was going well. I had recently received a promotion that came with a substantial raise and long-term financial incentives. My career looked successful on paper. So how do you think my family in Memphis thought I was doing?

They were proud of me, and they thought I was doing well. And that made it even more complicated. When I called home, they were so proud of me.

Oh my God, my baby, she's up there in Iowa doing well!

She's getting promoted.

She's meeting with the CEO.

And I was miserable. No one knew, not even me! I felt

like I was carrying the weight of my family's pride. They were proud of me, and I didn't want to let them down.

It's one thing to be fulfilled but it's another thing to have success. They aren't the same. There are a number of people who have success on paper, but they're unfulfilled in life. Never confuse the two as you journey in your career. Don't ever get so caught up in success that you forget what fulfillment looks like as it relates to joy and happiness in your life.

Success alone will not bring you joy.

I remember the exact moment I realized that the struggle was too hard, exhausting, unfair, inequitable, disrespectful, and dishonorable. My rhythmic beat was off, and I had given up so much of my authentic stride that I had become angry. And regrettably, I had begun to coach other women to acquiesce and change.

It was Black History Month, and we'd invited Lisa Nichols to speak. Lisa is a renowned motivational speaker, best-selling author, and life coach. We were sitting in the Executive Board Room, and Lisa gave a soft pitch of the speech she would later give to a broader audience. All our Executive Committee members were in attendance at the meeting.

I was sitting directly to the right of Lisa at the grand executive table. I had never met Lisa before, nor had I heard of her. At the time, I was the Chief Diversity Officer, and my team was responsible for the event. She and I were the only women at the table.

In the middle of her pitch, she stopped and said, "Hey, I need everybody to leave the room for a moment. Let's take a ten-minute break." Imagine sitting in a meeting where your guest says, I need everybody to get up and leave the room, including the CEO. Remember, this meeting consisted of the CEO, his direct reports, Lisa, and myself.

What in the world is she doing? Oh my goodness, did she just ask the CEO to leave the room? This is not going to end well. I am so embarrassed.

She then pointed to me and said, "I need you to stay." She could tell the leadership team was very uncomfortable with this request. Heck, I was uncomfortable.

Why is she singling me out? What did I do? I have intentionally sat here and not uttered one single word. What is she getting ready to do?

She said, "I just need ten minutes. Can you guys take a quick break? I want to talk to her," pointing at me. She looked at me and stared deeply into my eyes. She then ever so gently placed her hand on the top of my hand. She said in the most gracious and loving voice, "I don't know anything about you, but I do know this. You need to stop apologizing for who you are!"

She said, "When who you are and who God made you to be intimidates the hell out of them, it's time for you to give them the gift of goodbye. You owe it to your creator. I see your mask, and I am empathic to what I feel exuding from your heart. Give them *you* and stop being afraid!"

As I looked into her eyes and listened intently, the tears would not stop rolling. I cried tears of pain, frustration, and trauma but also from the relief of the weight I had been carrying. Lisa spoke to my soul. In just a short amount of time, she *saw* me. And it felt great to be seen and acknowledged.

Her words awakened something in me that needed to be ignited. Her words changed me. They liberated me and gave me permission to be me.

On this day, I made a vow that win or lose, I was going to provide corporate America with my authentic self, which is my best self.

I committed to doing the work as I knew this would not be easy. I would have to reprogram my mind to honor my voice and eliminate fear. I decided that from that day forward, I would show up as my authentic, beautiful self.

Lisa didn't know me, but she saw me. Our interaction was a life-defining and pivotal moment. Never underestimate what a word of encouragement can mean to someone's life, destiny, soul, and future.

Don't underestimate the power of visibility. When I left that meeting, she said, "Hey, would you like to go to dinner?" I invited her into my home and our time together changed my life. And throughout the years, she has always been available to invest in my wholeness whenever I need it.

As I did the work to find my Authentic Rhythm, I discovered three key strategies:

1. **Being Me is My Greatest and Most Effective Strategy.** Charge yourself to give the world your authentic voice because not only is it your best voice, the world is waiting to hear what you have to say if you dare to come out and be discovered.

2. **No Apologies Necessary.** Quit apologizing for being a woman, being different, being direct, and sharing your voice. The world does not want your modesty. They need your courage to SPEAK!

3. **Blend In, Not Fit In.** Your voice changes when you try to fit in, and you lose your message. The goal is to stay authentic by blending in, not fitting in! So many of us assimilate into organizations and cultures. Instead, we should integrate. Assimilation requires us to change. For some of us, the weight of this is too heavy to bear. When we blend in, organizations benefit from our authentic skills, knowledge, and experiences.

Rhythm Check: ♪ 🥁

When people feel culturally disconnected, it impacts every aspect of their life. It changes the beat and rhythm of your life. It is important to understand why you are in this state so you can move to the next phase of self-discovery in the next chapter.

1. Have you ever felt culturally disconnected? If so, when and why?
2. Do you feel like you belong at your workplace? If so, why or why not?
3. Of the four aspects of cultural disconnections, which did you resonate with the most and why?
4. Have you ever or are you currently feeling disconnected? If so, how did/does it impact your ability to feel valued and respected in the workplace?
5. How might you help others feel more connected at work?
6. How can you share what you learned in this chapter to reduce workplace exclusion?

Chapter 5: Finding the Beat

"Rhythm is something you either have or don't have, but when you have it, you have it all over."
—Elvis Presley

What's your authentic rhythmic beat? It starts with first being honest with yourself. You can pretend with others and wear a mask to hide your true identity, but you shouldn't pretend with yourself as you will never be fulfilled.

Search deep inside yourself. Do you love your true self? Do you have the courage to embrace yourself for who you are, not for what others think you should be, as complicated as that may initially appear?

What have you done to be accepted that is inauthentic, frustrating, or false to the very essence of who you are? Let's be honest. Most of us grow up wanting to be liked, loved, and accepted. For some, it started in our primary years. We relied heavily on the art of appeasing others just to be liked. This is even more magnified today due to social media platforms allowing us to like a photo, post, comment, or share videos. Social media has placed so much value on the number of likes or comments a person receives on a post. I have coached young women who have openly shared that if their post or photo doesn't get a certain number of likes, they will remove it. What is this new culture of being liked teaching us, and what impact does this have in throwing off our authentic rhythm?

As you change and grow, having an authentic rhythm and being true to oneself takes commitment and recommitment throughout a lifetime. If you allow yourself the time and space to listen, the answer to what is true for you permanently resides in the very center of who you are. Being true to oneself is being open and honest about your feelings, values, and desires. It also entails openly sharing your emotions with others, enabling your truth to radiate from you into the world.

There will always be outside factors that want to determine who you are and what your rhythm should or shouldn't be. Being honest with yourself and those around you is not an easy task. We each have distinctive qualities, passions, and skills that make us who we are. There is still time to change if you're feeling lost in your life, offbeat, or unclear about what steps to take next to be your best at work.

I have often asked myself, why was I trying to dance to the beat of other's music? Heck, I didn't even like the song or genre of music they were playing. I was trying to dance to a song or tempo that was foreign to me. I allowed others' perceptions or thoughts of me to change my dance. One day I realized this wasn't my music, and that's not how *I* dance! I felt and looked awkward.

Have you ever tried to learn a dance and had to over-focus on every little step? You may have had to count each step…one, two, three…and practice over and over. The way in which you had to focus made the dance uncomfortable, awkward, and not fun. Learning the moves became so difficult that you gave up. In contrast, think about the dances you enjoy. What are the moves that make you sway and snap your fingers because it feels good? It feels good because the beat comes naturally to you. It's authentic nature allows you to groove and move at a tempo in which you thrive.

Some of you may be in organizational cultures, jobs, teams or roles that feel off-beat. You come to work every day and perform at a rhythm that isn't your cadence. You struggle with happiness and fulfillment in your role. You change pieces and parts of yourself to be accepted. You are counting the time just waiting to get off because you are over-focused on every little step you make. You have observers watching and waiting patiently to say, "You did it wrong. Get back on the beat."

Truth moment…you are offbeat with your authentic

rhythm. When your beat is off, you want to quit and throw in the towel. Coming to work is no longer enjoyable. You tolerate your job. You aren't thriving. I've been there! Trust me, it can improve if you are willing to be honest with yourself and invest the time it takes to turn things around.

Let's review the necessary steps to finding your authentic beat!

You must first develop a close and trustworthy relationship with yourself if you want to understand your truth and convey it authentically. This starts with awareness of your thoughts, awareness of your entire body's experience, and knowledge of how you engage with the environment every day. Through reflective activities like meditation, yoga, and journaling, you can broaden your consciousness and improve your relationship with yourself. Through these exercises, you can learn to be more mindful and create benchmarks to determine when your actions align with your inner self and when it doesn't. You can be your greatest teacher if you invest in spending time with yourself. It gets simpler to self-correct when you are out of alignment as you practice more.

I've learned so much about myself that I was unaware of through the art of reflection and journaling. I began to understand what my triggers were both in my career and at home. I learned to be open and honest about my hot buttons and became more self-aware of how to manage my emotions better and not get stuck. It is not easy, but it is worth the journey.

As part of my self-discovery, I learned I had a trigger that showed up at work. It often caused me to get so upset that I would find it difficult to stay present in meetings because I was focused on pretending that I was unbothered when in all actuality, I was UPSET!

So how did I learn this, and how did it help me?

One morning, I was sitting at my desk writing in my journal. I started reflective writing with this statement: "Yesterday was not a good day at work!"

I'd written it without thought. When I read it, I wondered why. I didn't exactly know why I felt this way. I decided to flip through my journal to see if I had started other days in the same way. To my surprise, I found that same exact statement in several of my other journal entries. I then read those entries to understand what happened on those days. After a few minutes, I recognized one consistent experience.

WOW! So that's it. The journal entry I read shared a nearly identical situation that happened the day before. For context, I was in a talent discussion with other human resource leaders. One of the male leaders stated, "We shouldn't focus on hiring and promoting diverse talent. If we focus on this, we will diminish the quality of talent and compromise performance."

Throughout my 25+ years in human capital and diversity, I have heard statements and sentiments similar to this countless times. Over and over whenever there is a discussion on underrepresented groups such as women and people of color, the question of "qualified" becomes the overarching narrative. It is as if being a woman or minority automatically excludes one from being capable and qualified for the job. It infuriates me!

When I read this, I reflected on the journal entries that captured the statement. I asked myself, how did I handle the comment? Was I silent? Did I shut down? Did I leverage it as a learning opportunity? Did I seek to understand? My reality is that this comment, and similar statements, impact me in a way in which I shut down. I said nothing because I was so angry that I didn't want others to know. I thought it best to say nothing for fear of saying the wrong thing. I never inquired to learn more from the other person's perspective, and I never leveraged the situation as an opportunity to help others understand the impact of their statements. Instead of allowing this "hot button" to disarm me, I decided to rewrite my narrative and take a different approach going forward.

I made the following commitments and affirmations:

1. I own and acknowledge that depicting a women or minority as inherently being unqualified is a trigger for me. Own it. We all have them. The challenge is that when we don't know, it becomes a blind spot and can be hazardous to relationships, careers, and our ability to influence change and educate others.
2. I will no longer allow this to shut me down.
3. I will seek to understand.

4. I will educate and share how this impacts me and many others.
5. I will challenge this mindset with data and facts.
6. I will practice my response so I am prepared and effective!
7. I will continue to learn and grow because of these experiences.
8. I will offer grace.

These commitments are important in managing one's emotions in high-stress and high-stake conversations. The higher you accelerate in your career, the more this skill will be required to remain at that level and lead effectively.

Acknowledging this trigger allowed me to develop a plan and prepare. I researched all types of data on this topic including affirmative action data, whitepapers on the subject, books, and the company's internal data. In many organizations, I learned that women and women of color have the highest leadership effectiveness scores, education, and experience.

Months later, I was in a senior-level meeting and we were reviewing talent pipelines and management succession plans. We then pivoted to spotlight women and people of color. The conversation suddenly took a different turn. One of the more senior white male leaders said, "I don't mean to disrupt the agenda, but I am struggling with the concept of having a separate agenda item to discuss diverse talent. Why do we need to have this as an agenda item?"

The moderator of the meeting responded, "Well, it is because if we only went with the top three of four names that the business wants to discuss, there would be only one woman and no people of color. So to be inclusive and ensure that we are developing all talent, this is considered a best practice."

Now that was a great way to answer that question. Really nice answer.

The other leader said, "Well, I am really challenged with all this diversity stuff. I mean, if they were good enough, they would have been picked as the top people to discuss. By creating this process, we are inherently lowering the scale of talent to prove an inclusive strategy. I just think that when we focus on diversity and inclusion, we will begin to promote unqualified talent and go backward in performance."

I was the only person of color in the room and all eyes slowly turned to me. It was as if everyone wanted to observe how or if I would respond.

Joy you are ready for this, and you are prepared. Don't let them see your sweat. Put a smile on your face and seek to understand, listen, and then educate! Sis, you got this!

I knew this was a trigger, so it didn't alarm me, nor did it shut me down.

I waited a while because I wanted to see if anyone else would say anything. Too often women and minorities carry the burden in corporate America for responding and advocating on all things diversity, equity, and inclusion. We are silently counted on to represent our entire demographic. It is exhausting and overwhelming.

"Kevin, that is an interesting insight. I would love to hear more. What data are you leveraging to support your position and concern?"

The room grew eerily quiet! You could almost hear a pin drop!

"Well, I once tried to reach lower in the organization and promote a diverse woman to get some diversity at higher levels in my organization. I went against what everyone said and tried to do the right thing. It didn't work. So now everyone on my team reminds me that we tried and that it didn't work so I just think we need to be more mindful of not moving talent when they aren't ready."

"Kevin, I absolutely agree. Thanks so much for sharing but can I inquire more?"

"Sure, Joy."

"Have you ever had a White male talent that you moved up in your organization that also didn't work out? And how did that impact your ability to promote White men going forward? Did you see that bad hire or decision cause the same impact for White men as it did the one diverse female? I am curious to learn."

"Well, I mean…," he paused. "We have been doing our best to identify and help all talent. I really can't say it had the same impact. You raise a good point."

"Kevin, I've looked at our data, and it appears that our highest success rates have been with women and women of color. We must recognize that bringing new talent of any demographic to a higher level will always come with a set of unknowns. As humans, we will error and not always get it right, even with the best processes. We must not allow one or two examples to become the narrative for an entire demographic. Just as we give grace when White men don't work out in a position, let's ensure we offer that same grace to White women, Blacks, Latinos, persons with disabilities, early career professionals, Veterans, the LGBTQ community, and all the demographics who are counting on us to stand up and advocate for them. So, I highly encourage us to keep this process and discuss the talent that might not otherwise get discussed."

"Thanks Joy. You bring up a good point. I am in support of keeping it on the agenda."

"Kevin, can I be vulnerable and share how this conversation may impact others?"

"Sure."

"I once heard a story where a CEO met with the employee resource group (ERG) leaders to understand why there was minimal representation of women and minorities at the executive level. One of the leaders gave this response:

"Can I ask you three questions?

1. Do you believe when children are born, there is an overabundance of knowledge, skills, intellect, abilities, and perseverance that is **only** given to White baby boys?

2. If you said no to that question, then do you believe that women, people of color, disabled individuals, and others are capable of learning and growing?

3. Do you believe that women and people of color are capable of performing at higher levels?

If you said yes to the last two questions and no to the first, then you must believe that there is bias in the people making the decisions and/or the systems that allow access to the talent."

Kevin, this story has stuck with me for years. I share this in hopes that it has the same impact on you that it has had on me. I believe we have both unconscious and conscious biases in those who are making talent decisions, and we have challenges in our processes and systems that create inherent barriers for some of our demographics. When you say unqualified talent in reference to women and minorities, this is what I and many others silently hear: we aren't good enough, skilled enough, smart enough, educated enough, talented enough, invested in enough, or capable of occupying these roles. I know in my heart that you didn't mean this, but this is how it impacts so many of us. So please, going forward can we consider the impact of those words whenever we discuss diverse talent?"

And just like that, learning occurred in a safe way! But it takes courage, preparation, and wisdom. It's an art, not a science.

Being true to oneself is letting your uniqueness and originality shine through. When you adhere to stereotypes or social standards, you accept other people's perspectives as your truth. It takes bravery to be honest with yourself. You must be self-aware, truthful, impartial, and open-minded. It does not imply that you are uncaring or not respectful of other people. It implies that you won't let other people define you or make decisions for you that you should make on your own. Be as authentic as possible and conduct your life by your highest standards.

An intuitive feeling rather than a concept may frequently serve as the basis for determining whether you are in alignment or out of alignment. Openness, expansion, inner joy, and freedom indicate that you are moving in an authentic direction. On the other hand, if you aren't being true to yourself, it could manifest as tension, unease, alienation, resignation, emptiness, discontentment, or a lack of fulfillment. You can develop a solid connection to yourself and feel assured in knowing what is true for you by learning to pay attention to your deeper sensations and feelings and by creating greater awareness in your life. What is true longs to be said. Therefore, it is up to each of us to exercise bravery in expressing our truth fully and genuinely in the world.

Your model for authenticity, bravery, and self-awareness is your inner person or your inner self. It embodies all the characteristics that make you unique and robust. Make an intentional effort to become more in touch with who you are. Don't focus on changing, focus on improving. Opening yourself up to feedback can be unsettling because it requires vulnerability. Try not to let that stop you. Take time to consider the areas of your life that you would like to improve and use that as your compass.

You'll find a lot of new abilities and chances for development when you start to explore your inner person. Additionally, as your confidence grows, you'll discover more chances to shine, which is essential to feeling content and happy.

A second way to find your authentic beat is to understand your brand. One of the first assignments I give to individuals I coach is to understand your personal brand. What is a personal brand? Simply put, it is what people say about you when you are not in the room. It is the real you when you are not trying to be anyone else. It is how you show up in all settings at all times.

A personal brand is just that, it's personal, but it impacts your professional life and opportunities. It impacts your ability to be successful in every aspect of your life. It is how others see, depict, and experience you. Your brand is much bigger than a title. It's informed and enhanced by experiences, both good and bad. It's influenced by how you carry yourself, how you respond to things, how you engage with others, and how you manage your emotions. The positive news is that you can redefine and evolve your brand. It starts with intentionality. We will talk more about this in Tempo #4.

Let me introduce you to Kim. Kim was a young professional with big dreams and aspirations. She was a go-getter and tenacious in her pursuit to achieve her ambitions. She had a vision board and a career plan that was bold but also achievable. She met with me in hopes of understanding how she should navigate differently because she felt stuck in her career.

In our first meeting, I asked, "What do you want to accomplish in the short-term and in the next twelve months?" The timeframe of twelve months is key as you want to set a stretch goal that is close in proximity to hold yourself accountable. If the timeframe is too far out, many will lose focus and become noncommittal to their goals.

She replied, "I have been in the same department doing the same job for three years. I want to move to a different area to learn a new skill. Every time I apply for a new job, I get turned down because I don't have experience. How am I supposed to get the experience if I can never get the opportunity?" This is a question many struggle to understand.

I then asked, "Why do you think you are getting turned down?"

"I don't know. That is why I am coming to you in hopes that you can help. Do you think it is because I am young?"

"Kim, there are a number of reasons why you could be turned down. However, let's better understand your brand. What do people need to know about you to trust you in a job in which you have no experience? What are three things they need to believe about you?"

"Well, they should probably think I have high learning agility, I am a high performer, and I have the potential to do more."

"Those are all really good. Now how does that align with your current brand? What do you think your current brand is?"

"If I had to choose three things, I would say that I am powerful, I am a leader, and I am bold."

"Okay, those are good as well, but will those get you where you are trying to go? Based on your twelve-month goal, how useful are those sentiments compared to what you felt was needed?"

I then added, "Let's test your theory. Go and ask five coworkers, including your leader, what three words would key decision-makers use to describe you. Once you have all your answers, let's meet to discuss."

Exercise: Find five coworkers, including your current leader, and ask these three questions:

1. What three words would you use to describe me?

2. What is my top strength?
3. What would make me even better? (Now this question is where your greatest learning will occur!)

A few weeks later, Kim and I met. She started the conversation by sharing that she'd learned so much from such a simple exercise.

I asked, "Kim, what did you learn?"

"I don't know if I really liked this exercise, but I can understand why you had me to do it. Interestingly, there were a lot of commonalities in what people shared with me. Here are my top three things based on their experience: Kim is nice, dependable, and articulate. Joy, the last comment pissed me off. Why do people think it is a compliment to tell women of color that we are articulate? Can they find something else to say that speaks to our effectiveness such as, you are influential in how you build relationships and gain buy-in?"

"What else did you learn about what you heard?" I replied.

"Well, those aren't necessarily the things that will help me get the job. Nice is not really the top brand I want people to say about me at work. Nice doesn't speak to performance, capability, or potential. Is it possible to change my brand? If so, what should I do?"

"Kim, what did they share as it relates to what would make you even better?"

"Now this is where it got interesting. Can you believe they said I would be even better if I were more approachable? They said that sometimes, I intimidate people."

"Kim, I am not surprised by the feedback. Oftentimes, women receive this feedback. It is what we do with the feedback that makes the difference. The power is in knowing. Once you know, you can do something about it.

Remember when I asked you about your brand? You shared that you were bold and powerful. Think about it. How might you be over-indexing on power and boldness in a way that you are shutting down comfort? These are the things we can work on together to create a different experience so that we can change the narrative to work *for* you instead of against you. You need to learn how to win on your terms without compromising the very essence of who you are."

It is important that you understand how people experience you. It is critical to your success and future opportunities that you are clear about how you show up and align your presence in a way that propels your goals and aspirations forward. One of the safest ways to ask for feedback is called EBI. EBI stands for "Even Better If." This is a great way to get the feedback you might have never received, but desperately need to hear. It allows people to share what they may deem as "hard to share" information in a safe way. Just imagine that you worked extensively on a big presentation for over a month, and you thought you nailed it. When the meeting is over, you ask your leader, "How do you think I did, and do you have any feedback?" Which of the following is easier to hear, share, and understand in a way that keeps you motivated but also clear:

Option A: "You did fine."

Options B: "It went well but you failed to include an executive summary. This is a big miss and can cost you. Make sure you include that next time."

Option C: "It went well. Your presentation would be Even Better If you add an executive summary at the beginning to ground the listeners next time."

Each of us has the capacity and the desire to improve. To successfully stay true to ourselves and grow, we must have the knowledge and insights that can help us to improve. In Tempo #4, I will share a principle to help you stand out on purpose.

Rhythm Check: ♪ 🥁

1. What stood out to you in Tempo #2, Off-Beat?
2. Are you in an Off-Beat season in any area of your life? If so, what area and why?

3. Are you Off-Beat in your career? If so, why?
4. What are your trigger points?
5. What did you learn that can help you to improve when faced with your triggers?
6. What is your EBI? What would make you EVEN BETTER? What is getting in your way of achieving your career aspirations?

Rhythm Check-in:

Let's assess your current work experience. On a scale of 1-10 with 10 being the highest rating and 1 being the lowest, plot your Authentic Rhythmic Meter. Place a dot in each area and connect the dots.

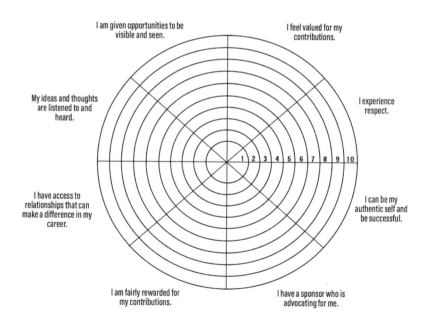

What are your reflections?

_____

_____

_____

_____

_____

_____

_____

_____

_____

_____

_____

_____

_____

What surprised you?

_____

_____

_____

_____

_____

_____

_____

_____

_____

_____

_____

_____

What is your greatest opportunity and why?

_____

_____

_____

_____

_____

_____

_____

_____

_____

_____

_____

_____

What is your most significant area of satisfaction and why?

_____

_____

_____

_____

_____

_____

_____

_____

_____

_____

_____

_____

TEMPO #3: RHYTHMIC-FLOW

Chapter 6: Consistency

"Rivers are places that renew our spirit, connect us with our past, and link us directly with the flow and rhythm of the natural world."
—Leo Tolstoy

Now that you have found your rhythmic beat, how do you keep up with the tempo? Imagine listening to a love song with a slow tempo, and suddenly, it switches to a fast tempo with no warning or transition. I love music and enjoy listening to genres ranging from slow jazz to upbeat gospel music. Often, I will play different genres of music back-to-back. My children tease and inquire, "How do you do that? Why don't you create a playlist with similar types of music? I don't understand how you go from jazz to choir music."

Now apply this analogy to life. Life will bring many twists and turns that we don't foresee. One minute, things could be going great, and the next, you receive a phone call out of nowhere that turns your world upside down. Take, for instance, these scenarios: *a) you just learned you have a baby on the way, b) your spouse just lost their job, c) your manager quit, and now you've lost your sponsor, d) you didn't get the promotion, e) you just learned they are downsizing your department.* How do you maintain your beat or rhythmic consistency when you can't control the music?

Rhythmic Flow

Imagine a flowing river with many obstacles, yet it continues to flow. The water permeates its intended path regardless of the current (the beat). It doesn't allow debris, barriers, or even people to stop its journey. You are that river, and that rhythmic flow is achievable.

Rhythmic flow is when you are clear about your mission and your objective. You don't allow the circumstances in life or your career to detract, deter, or disrupt your agenda. You remain steadfast, persistent, and consistent in what you aspire to achieve and attain. And just like that river, it increases its current when the weather conditions get stormy and windy. At times, the flow intensifies so much that it becomes dangerous for people who get in its way.

When things get hard in your life, you need to increase your tempo and become more vigilant in pursuing your goals. Whatever you do, don't give up. You need consistency, persistence, and diligence on this journey to achieve your rhythmic flow.

WHY CONSISTENCY?

The common misconception is that consistency equals settling. Being consistent does not entail giving in or continuing with a situation, relationship, or profession that is not beneficial for you. It doesn't imply that you must adhere to customs or principles others define for you. We live in an ever-changing world, and we need to adapt.

Some women will stay in unfulfilled jobs and call it consistency. No, it's not. To be consistent, you don't have to settle for less than you deserve. Find a new tempo if your current job or position isn't working or adding value to your life. If you are not being valued or appreciated, now is the time to create a more consistent flow that brings joy to all aspects of your life.

Success depends on consistency, which is a crucial factor. Consistency entails committing to your objectives and maintaining attention to the things and actions necessary to achieve them. Consistency means making ongoing efforts to carry out actions repeatedly until you reach your goals, which calls for a long-term commitment from you. Being consistent requires discipline, accountability, and responsibility.

Between failure and success is consistency. Any person who wants to succeed in any pursuit should be consistent.

Because of how our society functions and the widespread use of technology in today's world, it is easy to understand why many people get distracted and cannot succeed in their careers. The modern world is based on immediate satisfaction, and the presence of technology has increased people's impatience and desire for immediate gratification. People's thoughts about what they want to accomplish in life have gotten clouded by too many distractions, and there is a lack of focus, discipline, accountability, and commitment.

Success in anything we set out to do in life depends on the strength of consistency. Therefore, the first step to consistency is having a specific objective. Becoming motivated is challenging if you don't have a clear goal. If you're having trouble setting goals for your life, perhaps you might find inspiration in the lives and experiences of others. Set SMART goals. S.M.A.R.T. stands for specific, measurable, achievable, relevant, and time-bound.

As a young girl growing up, I knew I wanted to be successful in whatever I did. The truth is, I had no idea how I would do that or what I had to do to attain the success I desired. At one point, I was starting to feel despondent when most of my friends had already carved out a niche for themselves and had an idea of where they wanted to be in the next five years. So yes, I can relate to the sad feeling you get on the road to discovery.

Finding your place as a young woman in a male-dominated world is difficult, but it isn't impossible. Women have always worked diligently to achieve their goals and be the most excellent versions of themselves. Women have overcome enormous obstacles without giving up, and they have persisted and reached the top. Numerous role models exist today who continue to break down barriers and demonstrate that everything is possible if you have the right mindset, proper conditioning, and work ethic.

One of the wondrous gifts in this world is becoming a mother. Oh, the joy of motherhood! Having the power to bring a human being into this world is strength and power. It depicts how phenomenal a woman is. However, being a mother isn't all you are meant to be. You can be a mom and so much more. Some women fail to understand who they are and their unique potential before they enter into the role of a wife and mother. Don't get me wrong, not everyone desires to be a mother, and that's okay too. Womanhood is not uniquely defined through the lens of motherhood. Being a woman is multidimensional, and she has many layers, gifts, and talents to offer.

There are many hurdles on the road to creating flow. The biggest hurdle is self-doubt. You might wonder if you can achieve your goals. Your inner voice constantly saying things like: *Why do I even bother? I can't do this. Who am I deceiving?* Everyone experiences self-doubt from time to time, and it doesn't mean you're not destined for greatness. Instead, you need to take stock of your situation and reassess your priorities to realize your full potential.

Understanding your true self, values, needs, and desires is the process of self-discovery, and it's key to finding your rhythmic beat. Many of us lose sight of our principles and conceal our desires and preferences, even from ourselves. As women, we've made sacrifices, and in the process, some of us lost sight of who we really are or what we even want out of life. Deepening your self-discovery can change your life.

Don't imagine you can complete this powerful journey quickly. The process of discovering oneself never ends. It requires you to dig deep, look at every aspect of your life, and spend time thinking. To persevere in the process, you'll need courage and fortitude. When you engage in self-discovery, you might unveil truths about yourself that are difficult for you to accept. It's okay. No one is perfect. Self-discovery is not just an assessment or exercise. It is a life process.

7 TIPS TO HELP YOU CREATE A CONSISTENT AUTHENTIC FLOW

1. **Try new things and take risks.** It is easier to stay in your comfort zone, but that isn't where you will find life's fulfillment. Take significant risks. This means you will try something worth the potential failure. And when you do, do it with no regrets. Living a comfortable existence will not get you very far in life, and it won't teach you how to face your fears. In my experience, avoiding your anxieties will only enhance the possibility that they will intensify and

ultimately control all your decisions.

I want to challenge you to take on one fear each month. It might be a minor thing. For example, you might fear not getting the job if you apply. If you apply and don't get the job, you don't lose. Instead, you will signal to your company that you are capable of more and desire more. Going through the interviewing process will offer you the opportunity to meet new people in the interviewing process and help them get to know more about you. You will also learn how to improve the next time.

The only thing that counts is that you act and take a meaningful risk for your life and career. Make it a habit to become accustomed to discomfort.

2. **Recognize your strengths** and consider how to use them. Playing to your strengths is a powerful way to get noticed and increase visibility in the workplace—volunteer for things that get you seen by key decision-makers. For example, you might be a great party planner or organizer, but in your corporate job, you are an auditor. You learn that your department is thinking of developing a new onboarding program. Use this as an opportunity to play to your strength and offer to plan the reception for the event. This does two things. It allows you to work with a new leader or team responsible for the program, and it will enable you to demonstrate a

transferrable skill and excel in your gift.

It has the propensity to open a new career door and demonstrate your ability to do more. Most new opportunities I got in my career were because I raised my hand and volunteered to take on a role that the company needed. It most cases, it was the type of work others weren't willing to do. Raising your hand is a powerful way to build your resume and brand and demonstrate leadership.

Be deliberate in employing your strengths and look for opportunities to build upon them. Put your talents to satisfactory use. What if you could operate your own business using your strengths? What if you could leverage your skills to open doors to new career opportunities? How would your career improve if you adopted a more targeted and intentional strategy?

3. **Start keeping a record of your thoughts** so you can review them later. Journaling is great for mental well-being. Journaling helps you arrange your thoughts and gives room for clear reasoning.

I journal every day. It is an excellent way for me to release my thoughts and feelings. It also allows me to look back over time and see my growth. As a little girl, our version of journaling was the pink diaries most of us had. Most of them came with a shiny pen and even a lock as they contained all the juicy stories of our childhood experiences. So, most likely, you have practice doing this. Start today: Dear Diary…

4. **Do things that bring YOU joy.** A sad woman has nothing to discover except sorrow and regret when she digs deep. Find and create joy. We won't always find joy in our jobs. Some days will be good, and some days will be bad. When the days get long and hard, find things that make you happy. Writing this book is one of the things that brings me joy. What brings you joy?

5. **Ask for help.** Superwoman is not real. She is a fictional character that a man created. No one is an island of knowledge so ask for help when needed. If you have no idea what something is, ask. Even the religious books say, "ask and it shall be given, seek and ye shall find." If you don't ask or seek knowledge, you might never know. You mustn't be reluctant to ask for assistance when you require it.

One of the most significant errors women make when attempting to attain success in their lives is attempting to handle it all alone. This is a challenging task for many because it requires humility. Most of the problems you face in your career have been dealt with and resolved successfully with people in your circle. Step into discomfort and ask for help.

6. **Create routines that will help you achieve your personal goals**. Clear a path that moves you closer to your career goal and purpose. If your goal is to learn a new skill, start reading, taking classes, and practicing to gain mastery. Set up Google alerts on the topic in which you want to become an expert. I have over ten Google searches set up to daily review areas to keep me abreast and knowledgeable of my discipline. It also aids in my ability to have intellectual conversations on various topics.

7. **Celebrate success no matter how big or small**. Sometimes we are our hardest critics. Change your perspective and celebrate what is working, even if it is small. Life is not perfect, and you might not be where you want to be in your life or career. It's okay. Take stock of your experiences and the wise decisions you've made. Start praising yourself for your abilities, successes, and superb choices.

The journey to finding your authentic self won't be simple. However, the satisfaction you'll have when you succeed will make it a worthwhile effort. Many women struggle in silence as they strive to find their happy place while bearing the world's weight. Learn to accept yourself. You won't discover your authentic flow until then.

Above all, love yourself. You are phenomenal regardless of color, shape, hair, or stature. You are a work of art. Look in the mirror daily and appraise yourself. You need no validation from any man or woman. You are enough!

Rhythm Check: ♪ 🥁

Recap: Your authentic flow depends on staying consistent with your dreams and goals. It requires that you believe in yourself and focus on the things that bring you to flow. Keep moving, delivering, feeling, and most importantly, achieving. This chapter on flow helps you to determine your terms. You can't win unless you know your terms.

- What are your terms? What brings you to flow?
- What are the areas in your life that require more consistency?
- How are you continuously learning?
- Which tip will you commit to going forward?
- Which tip is most needed to help you obtain better flow in your career?

Chapter 7: Unwritten Rules of Success

"Rhythm is one of the principal translators between dream and reality. Rhythm might be described as, to the world of sound, what light is to the world of sight. It shapes and gives new meaning."
—Edith Sitwell

Have you ever heard the adage, "What you don't know won't hurt you?" Well, that saying is not true in corporate America. What you don't know *will*, in fact, hurt you. It is hard to obtain authentic flow and rhythm when you don't even have a playbook. When you are flowing in your career river on your raft, sometimes the waters will get rough and tough. Sometimes, you can't predict the weather or the raft's direction. Successfully navigating or winning on your terms requires wearing or having the following:

- Life jacket (sponsor) – Its primary purpose is to protect your life if you end up in the water and provide psychological assurance and safety that you have help. Whether you are an experienced swimmer or not, a life jacket is required, so is a sponsor.

- Helmet (mindset) – needed to protect you from a head injury if you fall out of the boat and hit an object or a rock.

- Oar (mentor) – needed to navigate the boat's direction and keep you moving.

In your career journey, it is essential to have a life jacket, which is a sponsor. They provide protection when bad things happen, or you make a mistake on the job. When you fail or someone doesn't like you, a sponsor is your safety mechanism that instinctively pushes you back up to the top. They have your back and offer a supportive perspective to help protect your brand equity. They ensure that your successes are shared at influential tables and they provide visibility opportunities where you currently don't have access. Sponsors advocate on your behalf when you are not in the room.

It's also essential that when you experience a career or life terrain that knocks you into the water, someone saw you fall, stopped the raft, and helped you get back in the boat. You need a mentor or sponsor to offer support when your flow gets tough. It happens to the best of us. You need to have confidence that when life knocks you into the water, you will survive, even if you are not a swimmer.

Most working professionals have experienced one of the following career terrains: layoff, demotion, failed project, non-inclusive leader, continued denial of interview opportunities or promotions, lower compensation when compared to others, lack of feedback, destructive team dynamics, bad boss, bad performance review, unreasonable work expectations, demanding priorities, and doing work that you hate. Things that knock you off the raft personally include the loss of a loved one, not fitting in, divorce, relocation, lack of family support, demanding home priorities, guilt, health issues, feeling left out, lack of purpose, financial struggles, sick child, politics, lack of inclusion in the community, and a global health crisis like the Covid-19 pandemic.

The helmet is meant to protect your head from injury. Most reading this book will have fallen or made a mistake at some point in their career journey. When you failed, how did it impact your mindset? Did the fall cause permanent damage to your confidence? Did you give up? Did it affect how you view others? Did you get a concussion? If so, did you take time off to heal? Did you give your mind the rest time it needed to heal from the trauma it experienced? Or did you take an aspirin and go immediately back to work? A healthy mindset is critical in obtaining authentic flow and rhythm. You must protect your peace and your mental well-being. What's the long-term impact when you ignore injuries to your mind?

The oar will guide you and help you pivot when you see rough terrain ahead. In a workplace setting, oars are our mentors. Everyone should have a mentor. Do not wait for the organization to assign you a mentor, find one yourself. Join networks and groups in your company to help expose you to more "oars." Oars guide you and offer advice to keep you from getting stuck or going the wrong way. It is important to choose the right oar. Your oar should be someone that has been where you are trying to go. They know the waters and understand the currents and the flow. They help you navigate and understand the rules to help you win!

Many of you have heard of "the talk" about race, but what about the "work talk?"

This is how it goes:

"Now, when you get a job, you must understand that work is work and personal is personal. Don't talk about your personal business at work. You don't go to work to make friends. You go to work to work. Make sure you do a good job and work harder than everybody else. Leave them no reason to want to get rid of you. Do your best to do everything they ask you so you can keep your job and make enough money to take care of your family. Getting promoted is a bonus. You will have to do twice the work even to get noticed. Promotions will only come to you if you are successfully excelling in your role. Then, and only then, will you get the promotion. Now don't invite your coworkers into your home. If they think you have anything nice, you will never get a raise or promotion. If you get a new car, don't drive it to work. You should have a work car and a personal car. If your spouse has a great job, don't tell them, as you won't get a raise! Remember, stay humble and be nice to your boss. Always know, the rules are different for us. You can't do what they do."

Growing up, this was "the talk" that I repeatedly heard. It's the talk many minorities heard as well. I was taught you only need two things to be successful in your career: a good education and hard work. This was the secret to being successful in corporate America. I believed in meritocracy even though I had been taught differently. I thought times had improved and individuals would be rewarded based on merit. So, when I joined the workforce, I did exactly as I was told. I focused on working hard.

A considerable part of the success equation was left out. Many people come to work daily frustrated because they rely on what they believe to be an unfair system. But what happened to the women's movement? What happened to Equal Rights and Pay Equity? Why do we still see women underrepresented in the highest corporate offices? Why are women of color the most marginalized and underpaid in corporate America? Why are Latino men and Black men still being left behind? What about persons with disabilities, veterans, and LGBTQ+ rights? Where are the laws and policies to protect all of us? Where is the meritocratic system we all dreamed of and were made to believe somehow depended on how smart and hard we worked?

Well, we focused on being busy versus strategic. Instead of working on the system, we were happy working *in* the system. Instead of advocating to change policies, systems, and cultures, we kept our heads down and focused on proving ourselves. We focused on trying to prove our worth. We wanted people to see our intellectual prowess. We were just busy. We were like the hamster in the wheel, working and working and working and going…nowhere.

Many of our forefathers worked in a system that never rewarded them for their work. So how will we win in a system that doesn't seem fair? To win any game, you must know the rules. The "Work Talk" focused on performance but left out two key and important areas, relationship capital and visibility.

To win in corporate America, you must master these three fundamental rules:

1. **Performance is the baseline**. It's 50% of the pie. Performance is non-negotiable.

2. **Relationship capital is a differentiator.** This can and will make a difference exponentially in your career. This is 25% of the pie.

3. **Visibility: They need to know and like you!** This is the last 25% of the pie.

So, I didn't know anything about the relationship capital strategy or this model. No one taught me that I needed to make friends and that people needed to like me as a person if I wanted to achieve success in my career.

I remember working in the aerospace and defense industry, and I was keeping my head down and focusing on delivering. I was lucky as I had an amazing leader. I am so grateful to have worked for someone who believed in me and took the time to teach me the unwritten rules of corporate America.

I had just come into his office one day for our bi-monthly one-on-one meeting. I walked in and sat down with my pen and paper. I handed him a printed agenda of what I wanted to discuss. I went straight into reviewing the agenda items on my list. He sat back in his chair and laughed at me.

He said, "Joy, just stop."

Bewildered, I looked at him because I didn't understand what I had done wrong.

He proceeded, "Joy, I appreciate your ability to be so prepared, but why don't you start with, 'Hi Robert, how are you today?' Or 'what did you do this weekend?'"

KEY TO SUCCESS

OKAY. Now, this is a very important person, and why would I waste his time talking about personal stuff when we have real work to discuss?

"Robert, I respect your time and want to make the best use of our time together."

"Joy, I like you, but I need to teach you a few things. I have no question about your ability to get the job done or to do a great job. But that's only 50% of what's needed. You are missing the other 50%, and that's what's most important in my book."

Now I am baffled. What is he talking about?

"Sir, I am confused. What 50% am I missing?"

"I think you are extremely talented, and I assume you have high ambitions and aspirations. Is that correct?"

I replied, "Yes."

"Well then, you need to understand the unwritten rules of success. See, performance is only 50% of the equation. The other 50% is what will differentiate you. We can hire people a dime a dozen that are great performers. That is the price of entry. It's foundational. To get to the next level, you need relationships. People need to know and like you.

Remember this: People don't promote people they don't know."

"Wow, Robert, what should I be doing differently?"

"Focus on the relationships and stop being so buttoned up. Let people in to get to know you."

This was the second most powerful conversation I had in changing my career trajectory. In essence, everything he shared was counter to what I had been taught and how I had been raised. He was saying I had to make friends at work. This was the opposite of what I had been doing as I intentionally avoided personal events. I didn't talk about my family to ensure I had boundaries between my work and personal life. I worked hard to be respected for my work, and now I was being told to spend time asking my boss about his weekend. This was difficult and painful for me to hear.

I remember calling my mom and sharing that I thought this was crazy! To my dismay, she encouraged me to try it. I then began to go into every meeting and spend a minimum of five minutes talking about what I considered "waste of time" topics to appear more approachable. I began to notice improvements in how people treated me. I got invited to the homes of people that had never seemed to take an interest in me. I was shocked.

Many are focused solely on the work and I was too. Performance alone will get you a satisfactory job, but relationships will get you a career. I remember Robert saying, "I don't know anything about you, but what you deliver. People don't promote people they don't know." He shared that people need to know you well enough to know that when major decisions are required, they know how you think. They need to understand your judgment and values. They need to see how you carry yourself inside and outside the company. They want to know personal things about you at certain levels, such as whom you are married to and your parental status. They want to relate to you. You can't build a relationship if you can't relate to the person.

Once you enter senior leadership, you are a brand for the company. Every time you are in a public setting, every social media post you make, and every event you attend, you represent the company. Even when you don't care to be, you are always on!

You are a brand the more senior you become in leadership. Your conduct can be measured in any setting and impact your career, whether you are at work or not. So, it's important for the organization to know and trust you as you directly impact their brand and business. And if they don't know you, you will have a more challenging time getting promoted.

Robert also advised that I needed to learn the art of small talk. This was the piece that was the hardest for me because it seemed inauthentic. I am not a fan of small talk, and it felt disingenuous to make up stuff to talk about merely to be liked. I just wanted to do amazing work and go home to my family. But at some point, I realized I needed to win on my terms! Now that I knew the rules, I could move authentically while still allowing myself to win.

As I reflected, I was focused 100% on performance and didn't do small talk at all. I didn't have a groove or authentic rhythm to feel comfortable engaging in small talk with senior leaders.

So, what is a groove move? When you are on the dance floor and hear the song you love, you most likely go to your staple groove. A staple groove is how you move, flow, or sway your body to the beat *you* hear. It comes naturally to you because it's *your* groove. It may look off-beat to others, but it is onbeat for you. People that know you well can probably demonstrate your staple groove or dance. In the corporate environment, you need to master your groove. You need to find your natural rhythm so you can win. Here are three steps to create your small talk groove:

Groove move #1. Observe the room and setting. What values do you see displaced?

Groove move #2. Research topics of interest to provoke dialogue and make connections.

Groove move #3. Find things about yourself that you feel safe sharing to help others know you better.

Groove move #1. When walking into any room or even a virtual meeting, observe the room. What do you see? If there are photos, who or what is in the picture? Do you see awards, pets, art, etc.? Leverage this as your starting point.

In most cases, people display artifacts in their office or workspace that is important to them. Leverage this as your conversation starter. People LOVE to talk about what they are passionate about. It will help start a dialogue that can allow you to learn more about one another. It can also help you appear more approachable and friendly.

Groove move #2. Research topics of interest to provoke dialogue and make connections. Working in the Midwest, I quickly learned that people love football. Sports is a big topic at work. On my first day of new hire training at one company, the facilitators wore football jerseys representing different teams. At that point in my career, I had never watched a football game. So, I started watching football because most meetings started with football conversations. I was new and didn't want to feel left out. I didn't watch the whole game, but I knew enough to contribute to the conversation. That's being strategic in making connections.

To develop relationships, you must be willing to meet others where they are and learn. Soon after this, I began receiving invitations to tailgate parties and games and I actually enjoyed them. I especially enjoyed the connections and relationships I was building.

Guess what? Work got easier. When you have an established relationship or connection, it is much easier to solve a challenging problem at work. Not only did work get easier, but I got promoted. People began to advocate for me and see me through a different lens because I engaged in small talk to help them relate to me,

Groove move #3. Find things about yourself that you feel safe sharing to help others get to know you. Every Sunday night, I reflected on small talk topics for sharing. Due to my upbringing of not sharing personal things at work, the topic had to be low-risk and safe.

I am a private person, and I didn't want a company's culture to force me to disclose things I wasn't comfortable sharing. This is how you win on your terms. You must play the game in a way that is comfortable for you. One mistake I often see made is that people think being authentic is challenging the game. If you don't like the game, leave. If you stay in the game, find your winning move and play to win. You must figure out how to build relationships in a place of comfort for you.

Still today, on Sunday nights, I pick my story to share for the week. It ranges from hobbies to my children. Everyone loves a child or pet story. Those are always winners and a place where you can find similarities. In most cases, avoid politics and controversial topics. Start with easy and lighthearted conversations to build trust. Remember to share but not overshare. Never share something that should remain private!

Rhythm Check:

Recap: You learned three ways to protect your flow. You also learned three unwritten rules of success—Performance (50%), Relationship Capital (25%), and Visibility (25%)— in achieving career mobility and agility. You've also learned three grooves.

- Which of these is your greatest growth opportunity?
- Which is your strength?
- What did you learn in this chapter?
- When you had a career faux pas, who saw you? Who helped you back up and brought you to safety? Or did you feel all alone?
- Who is supporting your safety and well-being?
- What is your action plan to win on your terms?

Chapter 8: *Sheet* Music

*"No two musicians will play the same music
the exact same way."*
—Joy

The music of life has a flow that creates rhythm. It is beautiful; it's rhythmic. It moves the soul and inspires the heart. When listening to a professional orchestra of musicians, it is a fact that no two musicians play music in the *exact* same way. There will be something different, even if it is not noticeable. They may breathe differently when blowing into the horn. They may touch the keys with an extra level of strength. There is something that is different and unique to how they play the music.

When you live your truth and operate in your gifts, your authentic rhythm, creativity, and musical ear come alive and flourishes. You may favor certain artists or musicians because they bring a sound, voice, or rhythm only they can give. It makes their artistry special. It makes them unique. Every musical agent is looking for a person with a different sound that hasn't been heard before. They look for a unique voice that exudes the "it" factor. Not only are they looking to hear it, but they are also looking to feel it.

You, too, were born with a special gift and authentic rhythm that only you can play or sing. Your sound is your power. It is your unique value. If you only knew how special you are, you would recognize that your best and brightest opportunity to win is when you are being your authentic self. It is liberating. It is musical. It is you!

Growing up, I was raised around many musicians in my family. They played every instrument, including the drums, horns, piano, organ, guitar, etc. And my family could sing as well. I remember hearing people ask them, "Can you play by ear, by sheet music, or both?"

There are two types of musicians, those who are classically trained to read music and those that can play by ear. Musicians that can read sheet music are more diverse as they can play practically anything. Their repertoire of musical styles is vast, as they can play different techniques and types of music. They are also better poised to play with other musicians as they can read the music to know how to accompany others best. Their musical sound is optimized because everyone knows their part and when to play. They perform better because the sheet music allows them to repeat, practice and memorize the music. This allows them to land gigs or jobs as they can play virtually anything as they don't have to know the music.

Those who know how to play by ear are considered by many as musical creatives. These individuals can hear and feel the music and make up their unique sounds based on what they hear and feel. You can be more creative when you play by ear and add your unique style or artistry. This methodology allows creative freedom as you can explore and test different sounds and rhythms.

Some might consider greatness as being able to do both. You need to be able to be creative but also know how to read the music. In corporate America, winning on your terms requires both. You must first understand their rules and how to read their music to win. When you are agile and able to play on any team, that's when you will begin to win. That's when you will get the next raise, or land the next job. Once you know the music and the song, you can add in your "flavor." You can allow your creative genius to shine and enhance the music. You can begin to embody your agency in fulfilling your dreams and passions because some agent (leader) is watching and waiting to find your genius.

Your winning strategy is enhanced by your ability to respect and understand how to read the "sheet music" of your organization. Throughout my career, I have been asked many questions to help people understand how to both read the sheet music and play by ear. Let's walk through some of the most frequently asked questions to help you know how to read the sheet music. Just imagine this section as a one-on-one conversation between the two of us.

Sheet Music Playlist
1. Conditioning
2. Confidence
3. Only is Lonely
4. Aggressive Tone
5. Hear Me!
6. Success is Not Distancing Yourself from Minorities
7. Mentoring Advice
8. Work-life Integration
9. Doubt
10. Women's Empowerment
11. Allyship
12. Imposter Syndrome

 Conditioning Sheet Music:

Why am I not being promoted?

There are a number of reasons why you might not be receiving the promotion or role you desire. In some cases, you might not have the proper conditioning or skills to achieve your aspirations. The first step in learning the sheet music is making sure you have the proper training and conditioning. The world is full of talented people. If talent alone were the only measure, every musician would be a star. However, that's not the case. Very few musicians become stars or create music that tops the charts.

The same is the case in workplaces. There are many skilled employees in organizations. However, very few will make it to the top leadership roles. So, what makes the difference? Malcolm Gladwell wrote in his bestseller *Outliers*, it takes 10,000 hours of practice to become a master performer or expert. If you want to excel in your career, you must practice, practice, and practice your craft. You must constantly seek new information to stay relevant and learn how to read the music.

You must do your homework and observe the people who have mastered the skills you are trying to learn. Seek them out and ask to shadow them. You need a great teacher and coach to help you understand how to navigate and deliver peak performance. You should seek feedback to understand how to improve and be the best at whatever you do. In some cases, you might be missing the feedback that is critical in helping you get better. Remember that feedback is a gift if you are willing to ask for it, hear it, receive it, and use it.

Confidence Sheet Music:

We often hear confidence is an essential criterion in the workplace. What are your thoughts?

Confidence is attractive both inside and outside of the workplace. When you believe in yourself, you signal to others that they, too, should believe in you! When you know you have the "it factor," people will treat you differently and better. Have you ever heard the saying, "You need to teach people how to treat you?"

When you act as if you belong at the table, people will treat you accordingly. When you sit in a meeting poised with a flare that shows, "I am not intimidated," even your adversaries will think twice about asking you a question. They will be hesitant because they understand the power of visibility when it's done well. They don't want to give you a chance to shine and show your value.

When you walk into a meeting, have an internal beat or a song playing in your head that makes you feel good, self-assured, and ready to show that you earned your seat at the table. What is your theme music? What gives you a sense of calm and confidence to authentically perform at your rhythmic pace?

In contrast, when you sit around the wall and avoid sitting in an available seat at the table, you are telling everyone in the room that you don't believe you belong at the table. Likewise, you are not exuding leadership when you choose to sit at the back of the room. Leaders are not afraid of the front row. Quite the opposite. They like the front of the room. It allows them to see better and to be seen. When you sit at the table, show confidence. Remember, everyone is watching. Show them the real you. If you don't believe in yourself, why would others in the company believe in you? If you choose to sit on the back row, why do you expect them to put you on the front row when career opportunities become available?

 ## The Only is Lonely Sheet Music

How do you deal with being the only person that looks like you on your team or in the room?

My grandmother once said, "It's hard to dream what you can't see." I've found this statement to be true in many aspects of life. The transparent answer: sometimes it is hard to be the only one, and it is lonely. The lack of physical representation of difference signals that you don't belong or you must be the model minority. Either way, it puts tremendous pressure on the individual to over-perform and serve as the role model for their entire gender or population. You feel different in a way that isn't always comfortable. You wonder why others like you aren't at the table. Many days you feel judged and alone.

You must reframe the narrative to win on your terms. You must first own and feel confident in being different. Differences can be amazing. You could say, "I am the only woman on my team or the only person of color. Did they choose me because I am a minority?" Let's reframe the narrative and say, "I am proud to be a woman on this team, and I look forward to making sure more women are on the team." Or "I am happy to break the glass ceiling for people of color and be a part of the team." See the situation as a chance to help others witness excellence in all its many forms. What if they chose you because you are a woman? So what? Men are sometimes selected because they are men, and we don't hear them whining, crying, or turning down offers.

Women, stop it! If you have been chosen, regardless of the reason, it's what you do with your privilege and opportunity that makes the difference. Take your rightful seat at the table and show them your authentic skills and talent! I once asked a top female executive if she would speak at an internal meeting. And she said, "Well, I don't want to do it because I don't want people to think you only asked me because I'm a woman. So, maybe you should ask someone else." I reflected on that. And I've heard the same for many different group demographics. Don't ask me because I'm an Asian woman, Latina, gay, or whatever dimension you identify. Let's rewrite the narrative and instead say, I hope you hired me for all my unique skills, abilities, and experiences. And guess what? You should leverage every aspect of who I am. If you need the woman to show up, I am here. If you need an inspirational leader to show up, I got you. If you need the life coach to show up, here I am. If you need a woman to show up, she's here, and she's ready.

Don't deny any portion of who you are. Show them what excellence looks like from your dimension of diversity. Only then will you give them the confidence to bring others along who represent your dimension of difference. If you are the only woman or minority on your team, let them experience your authentic beat, music, and creative rhythm. But don't stop there. Ensure you're not the first and last minority on the team. Help others and create pathways so other women and minorities can occupy a seat at the table. That's the pay-it-forward mindset. That's the give-back you owe society.

When I interviewed at a pharma company, I knew I would take the job because something extraordinary happened. While on the site visit, upon entering the escalators, a Black woman stopped me. She said, "Hey, are you new?" I told her I was there for an interview. She said, "Well, I hope you join the company and if you choose to relocate here, just know you have a family. We have a group of African American women, and we meet regularly. We would welcome you." Up until that point, I had never experienced working at a company where women of color weren't afraid to support one another for fear of the optics and who regularly met after work hours. That sealed the deal for me.

Stop waiting for organizations to create a community for you. Do it for yourself. At this organization, I had a sisterhood and community. Regardless of the demographics on my team or in my organization, I had my sistergirl tribe. When I needed advice or encouragement, I could call on this sisterhood. Even today, although I've left the organization, I still have the sisterhood. We are each other's sisters, and we are a network.

Many of you may be away from your family members as you've relocated for your career. You may feel lonely, but you don't have to be alone. Get involved in employee resource groups. They are a great way to meet new people and make connections. If they don't exist in your company, create your own informal group. Everyone needs a network to be successful.

 Aggressive Tone Sheet Music

How do you get your voice or view heard in a meeting without appearing aggressive?

Years ago, many of us were taught never to make a definitive statement in a meeting. Instead, form your statement as a question. We were taught to say things like, "Help me understand," versus "I disagree." You were never to call a person out and say they were wrong. Instead, you might say, "Help me understand your perspective or how will this be applied?" Telling in the form of a question was considered less threatening and recommended.

Still today, I use this method in high-stake situations and with people I don't have a trusted relationship. I use the following statements as ways to provide comfort and safety in the discussion and at times when I don't agree or understand:

- I would like to understand your perspective.
- Tell me more.
- Can you walk me through how you arrived at this decision?
- I would be delighted to hear more about your thought process.
- Are you open to ideas to make this even better?
- How can I help?
- I'd like to have more insight into this direction.

Whenever you start a statement with, "I disagree," it puts others on the defense and can create a hostile work environment. When people feel like they must defend or prove themselves, they lose the ability to listen and understand. It should not be about who is right and who is wrong. In these situations, everyone focuses on establishing their position instead of understanding the perspectives of others. This can contribute to you being considered as not a team player. No one wants to engage in non-constructive debates with members of their team.

When someone asks you a question in a meeting, don't be so quick to provide an answer. First, make sure you truly understand what they are asking. If you don't understand the question, simply say, "Tell me more." This does two things: it allows you to confirm what you think they are asking and gives you time to collect your thoughts and think of how you want to respond to the question. Most importantly, if you don't know the answer, be honest and say you need time to follow up on the question. It is a colossal mistake to answer a question you don't know. You will lose trust and the ability to influence others in the future if you aren't transparent.

 Hear me! (Sheet Music)

I am tired of keeping quiet in meetings and shrinking my voice when my leader is wrong. How do you deal with challenging your leader?

I was once told you could catch more flies with honey than vinegar. Some women struggle with being authentic and instead, they are passive. They are fearful that if they use their authentic voice, it would be like ringing a bell in a library. The sound would be loud, inappropriate, and disruptive.

Wisdom has taught me that the goal is not to be right. The goal is to be understood. And many times, we are trying to be right. Have you ever heard that old analogy, the pen is always mightier than the tongue? You will rarely win if you go against your leader. I don't care how much you try. They still have the power. In most cases, it's a losing battle. Don't try to prove you are right. Instead, try to be understood.

Help others to understand your view or vantage point. You will build more credibility by helping your leader understand your view rather than trying to prove them wrong. Most leaders don't want to be wrong, and some aren't even willing to admit it. This can be an enormous derailer to your career. Try to find common ground and have a one-on-one conversation, exercising wisdom in sharing your view.

Success is Not Distancing Yourself from Minorities Sheet Music

I was told my first hire should NOT be a person that looks like me. How should I respond?

Unfortunately, I too have been given this advice. I was mortified and couldn't believe someone actually told me that my first hire should not be a Black person. Sadly, many women and minorities have been given this advice throughout their careers. I have spoken with many women and minority executives who privately shared this advice caused them to exclude great talent for the sake of optics. It also caused them to assess women and minorities harder than White straight men.

When I was given that advice, I struggled. I went to my leader and asked for clarity. He said people needed to know I could be objective and include people that didn't look like me. If I were to hire a Black person, people would think I was only looking out for Black people. So, he advised me to hire a man and the person could be any race but Black. He then said, "You can hire a Black person later, but just make sure it's not your first hire or that you don't hire too many."

This type of advice is toxic and carries long-term psychological trauma for women and minorities. It toils their heart and mind as they struggle to understand the real message behind the advice. They have long-term regrets for doing what it took to help them stay successful when it was at the expense of others that looked like them. This advice creates a snowball effect, causing many women and minority populations to distance themselves from their own gender and race. It contributes to the following actions: avoiding sitting with them in the cafeteria, excluding them from after-work events, and not promoting them. It forces leaders to choose and deny their demographic for all the wrong reasons. It's a burden that minority groups should never have to bear. It causes you to believe that the more you distance yourself from your identity, the more successful you will become.

I often wonder, how many men have been told their first hire should not be a man? Or that they should make sure they avoid hiring and promoting White people? I would imagine a very small number, if any. I have never engaged with a White man who has shared this experience. This advice is septic and harmful to the success of women and minority populations. Just as you've been told they always hire the most qualified and best candidate for the job. You too should hire and promote the best talent regardless if they represent your demographic or not.

Women and minorities, please disrupt and stop this toxic behavior. You should always hire the best talent and the best talent includes all demographics. Do not exclude Black, Asian, Latino, LGBTQ+, and disabled talent for the sake of optics. Provide a fair and equitable process for all and this should not come at the expense of excluding others that look like you.

Don't be afraid to create connections with your community. Connect with others where you have similar interests, hopes, and lived experiences. Form friendships and work connections to help others who might face additional barriers in their career for reasons that are not fair or just. You have the power to change this mindset and your actions.

 **Mentoring Sheet Music**

How can I make the best of my mentoring relationship?

Leaders know when you're serious about your career. They can tell people who are driven, who desire success, and who needs help navigating the system. They can also tell those with no direction. Never go to a mentoring meeting unprepared. You need to come prepared to drive the conversation. You need to have more questions than answers. Come to the meeting with a problem that needs solving or a scenario you would like to discuss. Leaders love to help fix problems. So view problems as valuable additions to bring into a mentoring conversation. Just ensure the problems are not about you as an individual. The problems should be connected to the work.

Never come to a mentoring conversation with nothing to talk about. If there is too much white space, it's like being on a lousy date trying to find something in common. You need to come prepared to stand out on purpose. Every time you sit in a meeting, come prepared with your A-game and have your questions ready. When mentees are prepared, it excites the leader. It makes them want to help you more.

Work-life integration Sheet Music

How do you balance your career, personal life, and marriage? Is there such a thing as balance?

I had to get rid of the word "balance" because I failed for years. I no longer refer to it as work-life balance but rather work-life integration. Trying to separate being a mom, wife, sister, mother, life coach, friend, writer, and corporate executive was overwhelming and unrealistic. It just didn't work. I used to have a personal planner and a work planner. Trying to keep up with two planners was too much. I decided to integrate all my roles and use one planner.

I reflected and thought, "Is there a day when I'm not a mother? Is there ever a day that I'm not a wife? Is there ever a day I'm not a Chief Diversity, Equity, and Inclusion Officer? It doesn't matter where I am or where I go, I'm always all of those things. It was mentally liberating to know that I don't have to separate the layers of myself. I can successfully be all of these things.

Now, is it difficult for me to find time? Absolutely. Do I have days where I feel guilty? Certainly. However, I am very intentional when I say yes, and when I say no. This helps to protect my time.

To better manage my time, I wrote a list of priorities, and I began to reevaluate how I spend my time. Guess what? You will never outwork work! So, I stopped trying. I stopped pushing out things in my life that were important. So now I don't start Sunday evenings thinking about work first. I start Sundays thinking about my health. What do I need to do to protect my physical health, well-being, and my peace? Do I need to block time to take a walk or meditate? I start there first.

Second, I think about my relationships. Who do I need to call this week? Who do I need to check on? Do I need to go on a date on Saturday with my husband?

Lastly, I focus on work. How do I deliver excellence this week on my commitments that allows me to stay healthy and present in my relationships? This methodology is effective for me, and it is how I integrate all aspects of my life.

Doubt Sheet Music

How do you deal with doubt when you have been made to feel like you are not enough?

I have days of doubt and bad days just like you do. But what's the story that will move you forward? That's the story you need to believe. For example, if you were invited to an event, they could have asked you because of your gender or they needed a diverse candidate. They could have also invited you because you're terrific or because they want to invest in your development. Which one of those stories will move you forward? That's the one you need to believe. Don't ever believe a story that will make you stuck without validating its truth. If you don't have validation, give yourself permission to think of the best and most gracious story. That's what's going to move you forward. This is how you can combat doubt and move forward.

Women's Empowerment Sheet Music

What's the difference between women's empowerment and women's equality?

Let's unpack this a little bit. The word equality, at its core, means equal. So, let's review an example of what equality

158

could look like in a workplace as it relates to gender.

Here's one example. If you're hosting a meeting, did you invite men? Did you invite women? Did you have an equal process that allowed the same access for both genders? That's women's equality.

Women's empowerment is different. Women's empowerment means, did you provide the opportunity of success for women? Did you provide the conditions in which women felt empowered to be heard, acknowledged, valued, and respected in the same manner as men? Did you empower them and provide the conditions relative to psychological safety, where they felt their opinions were just as important as men? That's women's empowerment, which is different from women's equality.

I've been invited to a number of meetings and tables where I was not empowered to use my voice or contribute to the discussion. I was invited but not included. I was not given the support to feel safe speaking up or offering my perspective. Quite the opposite, I was told to not speak unless I was specifically referred to or asked. We need to empower women not silence them. We need equality, equity, and empowerment.

 **Allyship Sheet Music**

What are ways we can be effective allies for women?

I attended two conferences recently, one of which was dedicated to the very topic of women's empowerment. I've been an advocate for gender issues from as early as I can remember. I've been in the work environment for twenty-five-plus years, and we're still discussing the same things we discussed decades ago. You could even suggest on some issues, we are going backward. Allyship means I believe in you and cause you no harm. Advocacy means I believe in you and prevent harm from happening to you.

Did you catch the difference? For years, we've had many allies and allies can be silent. However, advocacy means I believe in you, and I will move barriers out of your way to ensure success. I will grab your hand and pull you along to make a way for you. This is how we need to support one another. I want to submit to women, I'm somewhat tired of us having conversations in which we ask men to be allies for us. I want to change this conversation because I think history would tell us they've done that in many regards. We wouldn't be where we are today without men. So, men, thank you.

The biggest challenge for women is we haven't done an excellent job helping each other. Today in the United States, we graduate more women than men in undergraduate degrees and more women than men in master's degrees. Seventy-five percent of valedictorians in the United States are women. When we look at performance data, women are high performers and highly ambitious. We're innovative, educated, and creative, yet we have not closed the gender gap at the highest tables in corporate America. Why is that? It's because we are still waiting on others to do it for us and we are afraid to support one another for fear of optics.

If you sit in a position of power and you have the opportunity to advance women, use your voice and use your power. Start with simple things that can pay off big. When you open a position or requisition inside your team, ensure that the people you interview are representative of women, women of color, persons with disabilities, women veterans, and women who identify in the LGBTQ+ community. When you create the interview panel, ensure it's not just men. Have women at that table when you are assessing opportunities to reward, develop, advance, and promote talent. Make sure you're looking at it through the lens of gender. That's what advocacy can mean, and it can make a difference.

When women show up as advocates and empower other women, we can change the numbers and make an impact holistically. We have the numbers, the smarts, and the skills. It's time for us to stop waiting on others to do it for us.

 Imposter Syndrome Sheet Music

How does one navigate and overcome imposter syndrome?

Imposter syndrome is real. Many women may wonder why I even put this in the book. But guess what? This is the reality of many women. It's almost like a fake voice in your head telling you that you are too busy, too old, and not ready.

Women are very effective observers. We listen to the actions of the organization versus the words. When you see men elevating faster in organizations than women, that's a message. It's a statement. When you see that women have to do the job before they're promoted, that's a message. That's a statement. Women didn't create imposter syndrome. Real life has taught women these messages. Women are graduating at rates higher than men, yet women aren't equally represented at the most senior levels of leadership. That's a message. That's a statement.

When you have aspirations to take on new roles or aspire to take on courageous, creative opportunities, those messages speak to you. They convince you the dream is too big or unattainable. And sometimes real people speak. When you share your dreams and goals, you expend a great deal of energy thinking about how others will respond. I remember one of the things I used to do in mentoring conversations. I would ask my mentor, "What do you think I'll be good at?" I don't ask that question anymore because it's my life. I talk to them about my aspirations. I look to them for advice because that's all a mentor is, an advisor. They have no skin in the game.

Get a dream builder in your life. Find someone that when you hear the imposter syndrome music play in your head, they will tell you, "Sis, you got this! Go forward. You are as ready as everybody else." So, put your name in the hat for that next job. You can't lose if you never start the race.

Rhythm Check:

1. What sheet music resonated most with you?
2. What is the sheet you need to learn how to read?
3. Which sheet music will help you the most in your career?
4. Which sheet music will help you the most in your life?
5. What sheet music will you include on your playlist?

Chapter 9: Strategic versus Busy

"Happiness is not a matter of intensity but of balance, order, rhythm, and harmony."
—Thomas Merton

I'm extremely busy! I have sooo much on my plate. I don't know how I am going to be able to get all of this done. My to-do list keeps getting longer and longer. There is not enough time in the day to get everything done. I wish I could get some uninterrupted sleep. Whew! I am tired of being busy!

These are the sentiments of women who struggle trying to be all things at all times to all people. Trust me, I have been there, and you are not alone. The rhythm of your life feels like it is on double speed. The music is playing so fast, you can barely hear the words in your life's song.

Have you ever asked someone, "How is work going?" and they respond, "I am extremely busy." Well, if this is your answer, this chapter is for you! Stop being busy. It's time for you to be strategic.

I received a phone call late one night from a lady I mentored. She said to me, "I need help."

I replied, "Well, how can I help?"

"I am applying for a new job but girl, I am so busy. I have so much on my plate. I wanted your advice on preparing for the interview."

I said, "Tell me more. What's the role?"

She said, "It's a leadership job. I will have an organization of about twenty people if I get the job."

I asked, "Why do you want the job?"

She replied, "I've always wanted to be a boss. I want to manage people. I think I am ready, and this is a great opportunity. What do you think?"

Again, I said, "Tell me more."

She then began to share a long and descriptive story where she named seven jobs and things that required her time over the next two weeks. Thirty minutes into her story, I stopped her and said, "Wait a minute. You are a generalist and not a specialist."

She sighed and said, "What do you mean by that?"

"A generalist is a person that has general knowledge on a myriad of things. Take for example a general doctor. They provide high-level counsel and advice on many issues such as a headache, toe ache, sinus infection, or a stomachache. Typically, you can get on a general doctor's calendar in two to three weeks. In some cases, the next day.

A specialist is an expert in a particular field of study.

They have knowledge in a specific area of discipline. It's often difficult to get on their calendar, sometimes taking months. When you make an appointment with a specialist physician, you most likely won't miss the appointment because you recognize the importance of their time. You understand you might have to wait an additional three to four months for a reschedule. And their time is more expensive than a generalist.

Busy people have time for everybody. They wear the title of being busy like a badge of honor. They've taught themselves that being busy makes them special or needed. They haven't learned the art of saying no. They focus on many things and achieve very little. People at work and home take no issue with asking busy people to do things because they like being busy.

I told my mentee, "I have three areas where I want you to reflect. First, a leader is a person that people choose to follow in the absence of power and a position. A boss is a person who uses power to get people to follow them. Think long and hard about why you want to become a leader. It is not easy. It requires a great deal of sacrifice, knowledge, and skills. You will be counted on for greatness of yourself and your team. It is a responsibility that comes with humility, compassion, and caring. You will need to influence others to deliver and achieve results while inspiring and holding them accountable. You will miss things in your life the higher up you go in leadership. There is a cost to becoming a leader.

Let's make sure you are ready to pay the fees.

Second, leaders behave as a specialist. They don't say yes to everything. They are strategic in how they give and use their time. They have learned the art of saying no. Do you know the one person in life who has no boundaries? It's a taker. They're going to take from you as long as you allow it. And as women, if we're not careful, we will allow people to take up every piece of our energy until we have nothing left to give.

Third, stop saying you are busy. Instead, be strategic. Have you ever heard a senior leader brag about being busy? No. They know how to manage their time, set priorities, delegate, and create boundaries.

If you don't know how to manage your life, why would a company trust you to manage their business? Your first leadership role is to manage your life. When you tell a coworker or leader you are busy, you inherently share that you can't take on higher-level assignments. You signal to them you are overwhelmed and barely completing your tasks. You are telling them, whether you know it or not, you aren't ready. What would change in your life if you were strategic versus busy?"

Think of life in a linear way and time as a concrete area that you can reframe. When you are strategic, you'll think about to whom you give the gift of time. I'm intentional when I answer the phone because it's my time. Just because someone else is ready to talk, doesn't mean I am ready to engage in a conversation. I politely hit the "sorry I can't talk right now" auto-reply on the phone. Where you spend your time can either deplete your energy, or it's going to raise it. Your mindset can be shifted in minutes based on who you are talking to and what you are talking about. As women, we give so much *of* ourselves but rarely give *to* ourselves. And one of the things you need to give to yourself is time. That's strategic.

Have you ever watched an eagle or seen an eagle fly? If you have, how many times have you seen three eagles fly together? Most likely, never. The eagle is a bird that lives in solidarity. It likes being alone. It flies exceptionally high, soaring through the sky with its majestic power and beauty seemingly effortlessly with its expansive wings, and its keen vision.

The first book I wrote was an unfulfilled dream for many years. Each year I would commit to writing the book, but I never did. One day a light came on and I realized I had the wrong approach. I was trying to do it by myself. I didn't want to bother anybody because I knew others were just as busy as I was. I didn't want to ask for help. I was trying to fly alone and figure it out by myself. I was operating like an eagle, trying to figure it out all alone.

An interesting fact about the eagle is when an eagle gets sick or hurt, there's no one to help it because no one knows it has fallen. The eagle does not have a team or support system to help.

In your low points in life, when you are stressed, maybe even depressed, having sleepless nights, most people don't even know it because you're an eagle hiding in solidarity. You want to be left alone. To the outside world, they think you're happy. The same is true in the workplace. Have you ever had a job, but you hide the fact that you hate it? Your family and co-workers think you love your job, when in fact, you don't like your job at all. Most of the time you feel you should be doing something else more useful or meaningful. You feel unfulfilled and stuck. Funny thing is, if you admit to the outside world that you hate your job, you'd have to answer to yourself as to why you haven't made a change. Women, we do that well because we serve everybody else. We're eagles. People see our beauty, strength, and resilience and they rarely see our insecurities.

Not only was I an eagle, but I was also another type of bird. I was a hummingbird. In contrast to the eagle, the hummingbird doesn't fly high. You usually can see a hummingbird at eye level.

Let's explore the nature of a hummingbird. A hummingbird is very protective of the family, the baby birds, the husband, the grandchildren, and the parent. It's so busy watching and protecting everybody else that it's just fluttering. It's operating and expending all its energy, yet it's going nowhere. It's busy. It's flapping it's wings so fast but accomplishing very little.

At one time, I was proud of being busy. I used to sing the song, *I'm Every Woman*. Do you remember that song? And then the commercial, "I can bring home the bacon, stir it up in a pan, and never let you forget that you're a man because I'm a woman." All these stereotypical articulations the world and media have put on us, and we're just busy and happy being busy. We are leveraging all our energy and time, not sleeping and going...nowhere.

For every appointed vision that's deep in your soul, the universe has equipped the people to help manifest it and be in your life. Learn from the eagle. You will never accomplish anything great in life by yourself other than being lonely. Get a team of people to help you. Don't be afraid to ask for help. That's the strategic beat and music you need to play.

Talk to people who can help you get the vision ignited. I want you to really think about who has been planted in your universe that can help ignite your vision. Now is the time to begin. Be strategic and stop being busy.

Rhythm Check:

This articulation of "being busy" is not strategic or a leadership quality. It puts the accountability on your circumstances, job, and family, and not you. Change the narrative and your actions.

1. Are you strategic or busy?
2. What do you need to stop doing to protect your time and become strategic?
3. What did you learn about the eagle and hummingbird that resonated with your current life?
4. What actions can you start today to become strategic?
5. Make a habit to stop saying you are busy when people ask you about your job.

"Busy people focus on tasks.
Strategic people focus
on relationships."
—Joy Fitzgerald

TEMPO #4:
RHYTHMIC-DANCE

Chapter 10: S.I.S You Got This

"A story needs rhythm. Read it aloud to yourself. If it doesn't spin a bit of magic, it's missing something."
—Esther Freud

RHYTHMIC DANCE

Life is an intricate dance. When you hear your favorite song, most likely, you move, sway, and dance without conscious thought or overwhelming effort. The excitement and ease with which you dance is the same energy needed to be unapologetically and authentically you. Fulfillment starts with being you and living with very few regrets. In your life, you are the main character. Once you have discovered your natural rhythm and mindset, don't stop dancing to the beat of your drum. Maintaining your natural rhythm will help you find more peace and serenity in life. It will help you become more productive and have a better chance of accomplishing your goals. Over time, you will become confident and self-assured in pursuing new possibilities.

Dancing is a liberating expression of what you feel. It's how you move, experience rhythm, and outwardly display expressions of what you hear and feel. No one can dance like you, regardless of what dances you have been taught. Your dance is an inspiring gift to the world. It exudes all the beauty and richness that lies beneath your surface. Stop standing on the walls of life watching others. Get out on the floor and move to your authentic groove. When you dance like no one is watching, it's infectious. It makes others want to dance and find their rhythm.

Most have experienced attending a party and either hopelessly waiting to be asked to dance or being fearful of getting turned down when asking someone. It's a horrible feeling. You are all dressed up and just waiting to be picked, selected, asked, welcomed or included. I remember once attending a party and feeling all the aforementioned feelings and fears. Then out of nowhere, a young lady enters the floor and begins to dance by herself with aluminous confidence. Everything about her rhythm, groove, and movement signaled, "I don't need to be asked. I am taking my rightful place on this dance floor and having the time of my life!" I was so mesmerized by her confidence that I, too, waltzed onto the floor and danced the night away. I then looked around, and the floor was filled with people no longer waiting but having a great time dancing to their own rhythms and beats. The moral of this story is that dancing to the beat of your own drum is not easy. It takes courage, but it's liberating. You, too, could be that example to help others get on the floor and live a fulfilled and authentic life. It's time to take the mask off and discover your groove and authentic moves.

SIS, YOU GOT THIS

I want women to know, S.I.S, You Got This! You are wonderfully and powerfully made. Greatness lies in you if you would only believe. You must choose to live now, this day, in a way that feels nourishing if you want to conquer your fears and achieve your aspirations. Once you free yourself from previous limiting beliefs, don't revisit them or allow them to invade your thoughts. When you liberate yourself, you can never entirely return to how things were. Liberation is a journey of being awakened and embracing truth and knowledge in a way that's freeing. It requires mental clarity and the ownership of your truth. The mind and psyche are powerful. Affirmations can be the fuel and catalyst for eradicating long-held fears and beliefs that debilitate progress in success. Let's start with this powerful affirmation: SIS, You Got This! Read this statement over and over again, and now say it out loud. SIS, You Got This! Start a new habit today. Every day, wake up and look in the mirror, and state out loud, SIS, You Got This!

When you see other women struggle or you lack sufficient advice or wisdom to help them navigate in their journey, simply say, "SIS, You Got This!" SIS is an acronym with powerful statements to help you stay focused and confident in your mission.

S.I.S stands for:

Stop the noise

Invest in relationship capital

Standout today on purpose

Let's start with the first S. *Stop the noise!* Kill the negative self-talk. Drown out the rhetoric that is telling you it's too late. You don't have enough time. You are too busy. You can't do it. You won't be successful. You are too old. You are too young. You are not ready. You are not good enough. No one believes in you. You must shut the voices or thoughts in your mind telling you that you are not enough. You are enough, and you are more than enough. ENOUGH!

It is not too late to accomplish your dreams. It is not too late to pursue your passion. You can get that next job or next promotion. You can be successful and win in corporate America. Stop the negativity that is immobilizing your dreams, even if it's people around you. Here is one tip you should write down and put in your planner, journal, cell phone, or somewhere that you visit daily: Stop telling negative people your aspirations.

Most importantly, stop asking people who you should be when you grow up. I often coach women who ask my opinion about what they should be doing in their careers and lives. While I applaud their desire to seek my input, I am not all-knowing or psychic. I don't have the answers to your life's purpose. The answers lie in you.

I, too, made this mistake. Early in my career, I often asked my leader or mentor, "What's the next role I should pursue?" I would be insulted and offended if their answers were too basic or mediocre based on my ambitions. In all honesty, it wasn't their question alone to answer. The accountability of both the questions and answers belongs to you and only you. Many seek confirmation from others. The process of seeking validation from others will often confuse and misdirect you instead of guide you. Follow the steps in Tempos 1 and 2 to guide you through a technique for revealing the answers you need.

We are surrounded by armchair critics who watch and judge our every move. Lean back and give them something to watch. Far too many people take advice from non-doers and non-achievers. Those individuals can only advise you on how *not* to succeed. Do not allow them the space and energy to rob you of your dreams. These individuals should be credited for all the innovative ideas, gifts, and talents that are buried in graves all across the globe.

There is a permission you give people when you share your dreams. Stop permitting people to limit your life. They don't deserve that power. Stop listening to the noise, whether it is your spouse, boss, friend, or family member. The noise is killing your vibe and groove. Moreover, it inhibits your authentic rhythm.

I stands for ***Invest in relationship capital.*** This is a career differentiator. Relationships are vital in advancing anything in life. Relationships can help you achieve your goals faster and with less stress. Remember, focusing only on performance will keep you on the job, but you most likely won't get the career you desire without relationships.

Be in the company of excellent and inspiring people. Having a friend or mentor who inspires you to dream bigger is crucial. Ensure you are in the company of people who are driven to succeed and drive you to achieve. Encircle yourself with successful individuals by seeking them out. Never undervalue the significance of achievement in your immediate surroundings. Remember that you need to be among individuals who inspire you to achieve your goals. Positive people will help you learn how to become more optimistic and work toward your objectives.

Create a personal board of directors. This group should serve as advisors of your life's core areas that need rhythm. These individuals should have demonstrated success in achieving what you desire to succeed. For example, my personal board of directors consists of a life coach, a minister, a corporate executive, a working mom, a writer, and my husband. They are my role models. They keep me grounded and committed. They provide clear instructions and advice in navigating life and corporate America. They are my safe

"Stop giving others access to the volume button on your life. They will turn down the music on your dreams."
—Joy Fitzgerald

space and inspiration to stay the course regardless of the circumstances. They provide wise counsel to aid in winning on my terms.

Board of Directors are people who are well connected and influential. Please note that they don't have to be people that live in your city or individuals you talk to daily. Instead, they are people you periodically check in with. These are individuals who, when you need direction and when you need advice, can help. Find people who have accomplished what you want to achieve. Those are the individuals who are best suited to offer you advice.

A person who doesn't have a vision will be extremely limited in telling you how to obtain your goals. A personal Board of Directors can connect you with strategic partners to which you currently don't have access. They should be aware of your aspirations to offer strategic guidance. They should also make you aware and help you discover if you are getting off-beat. They will hold you accountable for activating your authentic rhythm.

The last **S** stands for *Standout on purpose*. The goal in your career is to stand out, not stick out. Be intentional and always stay ready. Have you ever heard the saying, "stick out like a sore thumb?" Merriam-Webster's dictionary defines this as being very noticeable in usually a wrong way. In the corporate work setting, sticking out is not optimal for success. It generally means you defy the norms in an unacceptable way. You portray or display behaviors that don't align with the organization's culture. Sticking out will inherently derail career opportunities. It will impact your ability to get optimal raises, superb performance ratings, promotions, and new roles.

In contrast, you want to stand out. Standing out on purpose requires intentionality. It is taking the time to create your life's playlist of songs, so you are strategic in playing the music and rhythm that helps you win. It requires diligent thought and strategic intent. You must listen to the music and determine what gives you energy, joy, and fulfills your purpose and your *why*. You should be prepared and thoughtful about how to stand out in every meeting and new connection. Remember, it's hard to promote or help people you don't know.

I often hear from mentees about their desire for new career opportunities. They want to obtain new roles and get promoted quickly. They want raises, and they desire to make six figures. They want visibility opportunities and to be noticed for their efforts. When they share their desires, I often ask, "What are you doing to stand out on purpose? What is your intentional move or groove?"

In most cases, they have no answer. They are unknowingly stuck. They are waiting for life to happen instead of being strategic and intentionally making it happen. They are waiting for someone to tap them on the shoulder to guide their next move. How many of you have been waiting to be tapped on the shoulder? You've been silently waiting to be seen and noticed. You are anxiously waiting for someone to tell you that you are ready and that it is your time to receive the next role, assignment, project, or promotion. Unfortunately, being tapped is not the strategic groove move! You have the power and the capacity to win if you become more purposeful and intentional in your actions.

One of the ways in which you can stand out is by being noticed in a positive way. Start by reframing your mindset on how you get work done. Many people struggle in their careers because they merely focus on "the what" instead of "the who." They create exhaustive to-do lists that encompass tasks to get work done. To stand out on purpose, you must know that "the who" is how you get "the what" done. That's the strategic dance move. That's the groove that will get you noticed, and others will then begin to dance with you.

On page 180 you will find a tool to help you reframe your mindset. Standing out on purpose requires visibility and relationships with your team, peers, key stakeholders, and key decision-makers. This tool is a compelling resource in helping you think differently and become more intentional. If you use this tool effectively, you will be better positioned to win differently in your career and possess the skills and relationships to win on your terms. This is how you impressively dance to your authentic rhythm.

Throw away that long exhaustive list of tasks and use this to get the list accomplished. Once a week, level this tool to help you think differently and stand out on purpose. Being successful in corporate America requires performance. You are already killing it. (If not, that's your first step.) You've mastered performance. You are missing visibility and relationship capital. Now you have the tool to help you WIN! I believe in you.

Wining with relationship capital and visibility requires that you focus on four types of people:

1. **Key Stakeholders** – these are individuals that will help you stay relevant. They may or may not hold senior-level roles, but they are very influential with key decision-makers. Their opinions matter. These individuals need to be talking about you in the rooms you don't have access to for all the right reasons. In some organizations, it might be the executive assistant of your function's leader. It could be a close colleague or person on their staff. These individuals know the answers to the questions that can help you. They know the unwritten rules of success and may have even written the sheet music in your company.

2. **Key Decisionmakers** – These are individuals that will make the decisions on who gets hired, promoted, fired, laid off, and given new work assignments. They are the individuals with the formal and informal power in your organizations. These individuals should know who you are and what you can deliver. They also need to like you enough to not stand in your way for new career opportunities.

3. **Colleagues** – these are your team members or people that report to you. These are the people you spend the most time with, and they can help you get exceptional work done. These are also the people you should engage with often and with whom you should partner.

4. **Peers** – this is a group many oftentimes neglect building relationships with because you see them as your competition. Develop effective and productive relationships with your peers. You need to have visibility into what they are thinking and feeling. They have the ear of your leader, and it is important to understand what they are sharing about you. One day, they too could become your leader. You can learn valuable information from them. Establishing connections with this group is a powerful beat to add to your tempo.

Rhythm Check:

1. What can you do to build relationship capital?
2. How will you increase visibility in the organization?
3. What group in the relationship capital model is your greatest strength? What is your greatest area of improvement?
4. What did you learn about yourself in this chapter?

WINNING WITH RELATIONSHIP CAPITAL & VISIBILITY

RELATIONSHIP CAPITAL

KEY STAKEHOLDERS
"How to Stay Relevant"

- ☐ Who needs to know about me for my career to advance?
- ☐ Who has insights that can help me win?
- ☐ Who can help increase my brand equity?
- ☐ What relationships are critical for my success?

KEY DECISION MAKERS
"How to Be Successful"

- ☐ Who owns the decision for the advancement of my career?
- ☐ Who needs to believe in me or like me?
- ☐ What do they need to know about me?
- ☐ What are the key moments that will matter in advancing my career?

COLLEAGUES
"How to Pay it Forward"

- ☐ Who is struggling on the team?
- ☐ Who do I need to check on?
- ☐ Who needs my attention or presence?
- ☐ Who needs encouragement? Or coaching?

PEERS
"How to Execute Flawlessly"

- ☐ Who has done this before and can help me?
- ☐ Who needs to be informed of my work?
- ☐ Who feels left out?
- ☐ Who can derail my work?
- ☐ Who can help advance my work?

VISIBILITY

Chapter 11: Stay Ready

"I know that once I get a good rhythm and a good feel,
no one can stop me."
—John Starks

STAY READY

Life is challenging and ever-changing. It's like the music on your playlist. No song plays forever unless you keep it on repeat. The music changes, and so does the tempo and beat.

In your career, you will face new challenges regularly. Some will help you develop and rise to higher levels. Others may detract your confidence and leave you feeling stuck. If you remain prepared and stay ready, you can successfully demonstrate agility and navigate tempo changes and different beats as they arise. You won't be caught off guard nor forced to alter who you are to remain relevant in the workplace. Staying prepared will allow you to adapt and adjust quickly. The phrase "stay ready vs. get ready" means you must be indispensable in the workplace.

So, let's address being indispensable in your career. What does being indispensable mean? Two words: absolutely necessary. You must be absolutely necessary in your job, work environment, entrepreneurial efforts, with your peers, leader, and team, or wherever you seek fulfillment. I want you to be indispensable in every aspect of your career or aspect of life that matters to you.

Here are **four key principles** of what being indispensable means.

1. You are counted on for greatness.
2. You have a recipe for success that cannot be duplicated.
3. You have an asymptote mindset.
4. You exude confidence in asserting your voice.

Number one, being indispensable means being counted on for greatness. It means that you consistently deliver in everything you do. Think about your team. Who are the go-to people that pull the weight, not only for themselves but they pull the weight for the entire team? When you are indispensable in business, you are a go-to person. You are a name and an individual that is top of mind for people around you. I remember when my daughter was in competitive dance. When she first started, she wanted to be in the front row. The person on the front row carries the team when you're competing. She often asked, "What can I do to be on the front row?" I would respond, "To be on the front row, you're the individual who practices relentlessly when new skills are taught. You raise your hand to try new things and volunteer. You're willing to put in the extra work and effort to help your team achieve at a greater level. You help others become better, and you listen to coaching and feedback. And when you hit the stage, leave it all on the floor and have fun."

Think about your current role. Are you the one that's raising your hand to take on the assignments no one else wants? Are you putting in the extra effort? Do you exude a level of discipline? Do you pull the weight, not just for yourself, but for others as well? To be indispensable, you need to be counted on for greatness for yourself and others.

Number two, you need a recipe that cannot be duplicated. One of my favorite desserts is a red velvet cake. I'm always looking for a great red velvet cake on significant holidays or potlucks. I once had someone on my team that made the best red velvet cake I had ever tasted. One day, I decided to replicate his recipe and make it for my family on Thanksgiving. I got the recipe's specifics and bought all the items I naively thought were needed for success. I was elated and ready to wow my family with my version of this amazing cake.

Unfortunately, I made the cake three times, and it was horrible. My attempt at replicating this recipe was an epic failure. Finally, I relented on the task at hand and gave up. It's okay to know what's your thing and what is not your thing. I pondered over and over why I couldn't get the outcomes I desired in making the cake. I realized that *who* makes the cake is an essential factor. They had specific tools and techniques I did not have. I had the recipe. I followed the directions as I interpreted them, but there was a unique value proposition I didn't have. I could not replicate or duplicate the owner's recipe. There was something special about their insight, judgment, and how they operated in making the cake in the moment that could not be duplicated by me.

If you want to be indispensable in your career, you need to possess a unique value that only you can bring. And even when others try to replicate what you do, it doesn't look like how you do it. It's not as effective or successful. Your authentic nature can't be replicated or duplicated even if you share the recipe. It is something special about how you move, operate, and exercise judgment in the moment that can't be taught.

One of the things that made me indispensable was that I raised my hand for the tough jobs. I volunteered for the challenging assignments, the tough work that most shied away from. It wasn't easy, but anything worth having is never easy. So, to be indispensable, don't sit in the seat of comfort. Don't live in a space of complacency. You must be willing to lean into uncomfortable places and do the work of such high value that you'll be tested to a point that forces growth and learning. You need to be the person people come to for that secret recipe in your workplace that can't be replicated.

Number three, you need to have an asymptote mindset. If you remember back in high school or college geometry, an asymptote is a straight line that tries to approach a curve. But when it tries to approach the curve, it never quite meets it. It continues to elevate and aim high because its goal is mastery.

The world is not static and life is not static. Careers and jobs are ever-changing and evolving now more than ever. The global pandemic that catapulted in 2020 taught us, if nothing else, that we can't plan for tomorrow. You must be agile and ever-evolving to stay indispensable and relevant. Take time to think about how you consistently and intentionally evolve. How do you continue to achieve mastery given your current environment, even if you never fully reach your desired end point? You should focus on the future climate you will one day face.

I remember asking a board member, "How do you interview a prospective CEO? What are some of the questions you ask?" The board member replied, "There are only two questions I ask. Your resume speaks to your skills. It speaks to your accomplishments. It speaks to your experiences. What I want to know most is how the person thinks and stays relevant. Here are the two questions I ask. First, what's the last book you read and why? And the second question is, what do you read daily that expands your way of thinking, challenges your ideas, and keeps your skills at that readiness level to predict and prepare for the future?"

If you want to stay indispensable in your career, you need to be continuously learning. Your thought equity and how you approach knowledge will become much more critical than the tasks you accomplish. Start by setting Google alerts. Set Google alerts on your career discipline or areas where you want to be a thought leader. Set aside 15 minutes in your day to peruse your alerts and read them. This is a free and effective way to curate content to help you stay current and relevant. You need to read something weekly that keeps you current and aware of growing trends and skills. You need to be the individual on your team that people go to for thought equity and leadership. Aim to be the individual that people come to because your knowledge is broad yet narrow and specific, where it needs to be, where it matters, and where it counts.

Lastly, stop apologizing and be confident in asserting your voice. Women, stop apologizing for your talent and ideas. I often hear women, for lack of a better term, dumb down their ideas in meetings or apologize for a different view or opinion. I want you to own your ideas, gifts, and intellect. Demonstrate your talents and your skills unapologetically.

It's powerful, inspiring, and it's the gift you were born to give the world. Don't minimize it. Don't apologize for it, and don't shy away from your talent or your gift because you think it's too big for others or you think it might make you appear arrogant. Confidence is a necessary form of humility. Organizations don't place accountability and responsibility in the hands of people who doubt themselves. Quite the opposite, they look for confident leaders. Humility lives in the seat of being grateful. Giving the world the best of you is a gift, and that is humility.

Finally, you need to know your worth in business. You need to know that you bring value. You bring a secret recipe that only you can give to your company and the world. You need to have a mindset where you are continuously learning. Learning is not a destination. It's a journey. If there's breath in your body, you should be seeking to learn, evolve, and grow. That's how you'll be indispensable. If you're like me, I would never go to a physician's office, a clinic, or even have my carpet cleaned by someone with no new knowledge. Imagine a surgeon who hasn't sought out knowledge in twenty years. Would you want that individual performing surgery on you? Think of the work you do from that vantage point. How are you staying competitive and relevant in your career field to make you indispensable and a top choice?

Rhythm Check: ♪ 🥁

1. How are you absolutely necessary at your organization?
2. How can you become indispensable?
3. What area of improvement is your greatest opportunity to standout on purpose?
4. Where can you strategically add learning to your routine?
5. What did you learn about yourself while reading this chapter?
6. What is an area in which you find yourself less confident where you know you can actually shine?

TEMPO #5:
RHYTHMIC- SOUND

Chapter 12: Slay in Your Own Lane

"The first lesson I've learned is that no matter what you do in your life, you have to figure out your internal rhythms - I mean, what works for you doesn't necessarily work for your friend."
—Hillary Clinton

RHYTHMIC SOUND

The word rhythm comes from the Greek verb rhythmos, which means "to flow." Everything in life has a rhythm, and your life has its distinct flow, much like the regular beat of your heart.

SLAY IN YOUR LANE

You are the composer of your rhythmic music. You are a goddess with irrevocable beauty and a great mind. Everything about you is a work of art and music. Why aim for perfection when your authentic self is more than enough?

No one can out-slay you in your lane when you live in your purpose. You walk with confidence that says, "I am happy with me." When you walk, you sway your hips from side to side in a fashion that embraces everything beautiful about who you are. You are signaling to the world that "I love myself." When you stride in your lane, your inner worth, value, and beauty shine so brightly that spectators need to wear sunglasses. You are authentically you. Your rhythm and beat play so harmoniously that you want to sing and dance to your life's music.

When you are in your groove and lane, you might lose people you thought were your friends. You might find that your circle becomes smaller. You might even hear comments like, "Now that you have gotten that big promotion, you are big time now. You don't have time for the little people." These types of sentiments can be hurtful. In most cases, your success is a challenge for the individual sharing those comments with you, versus you.

When you hit your authentic stride, everyone in your life won't be able to *grow* and go with you. It's okay. Many struggle with this concept. Some of your accomplishments will cause others to treat you differently. I went to my daughter for advice on this issue. She said, "Mom, when you plant a seed in the ground and it grows, it's called a flower. Everything possible was in the seed. When it grows as a flower, it didn't change its primary composition. If you planted gardenia seeds and it grew into a gardenia flower, the composition didn't change." She went on to politely add,

"You didn't change. You are still the same flower. **They just can't handle your bloom.**"

🎤 Everyone won't be able to handle your bloom but slay anyway! Do not shrink yourself or your achievements for others. You can be simultaneously humble and proud.

11 TIPS ON SLAYING IN YOUR LANE

1. **Stop competing with others.** Instead, compete with yourself. You are in a one-person race. Your success is not dependent on beating out the next person. It is dependent on you finishing your journey. It's enhanced by you running in your stride, your tempo, and your pace. So many people get distracted by what's happening in the next person's lane. You were okay with your race (your job) until you saw how someone else was running. You envy their promotion, their accolades, and their accomplishments. If you genuinely want to slay in your lane, you should learn to compete with yourself and stop caring about the achievement of others.

   You cannot beat anyone else at their race. Envying others will cause you to lose your race and miss out on your goals and aspirations. It will cause you to stumble and lose focus on your dreams. You were okay with your job and the amount you were being paid until you saw your peer get promoted or learned they made more than you—set goals based on your dreams, not others.

2. **Put an end to comparing yourself to others.** Do you compare your success to those you follow on social media? Or do you compare yourself with your girlfriends, coworkers, siblings, or college peers? Making parallels is natural, according to the social comparison hypothesis. However, it's unrealistic and unhealthy to judge your life based on others. It forces you to lose focus on your authentic nature. You lose sight of your lane and your aspirations. Please know that when you compare yourself to others, you are making a comparison from a minimal view. Social media shows you the best and most inflated versions of a person's life. There are filters and backgrounds that can alter the look, background, and even the setting. You only see the 20%. You have no idea of the "real" person or the struggles they've gone through to reach their success. You don't know their story! Stay focused on *your* lane. No one can outrun or slay you in your lane. Keep a gratitude notebook to help you remember the blessings in your life and as a reminder that your lane was made just for you.

3. **Be resilient.** Each journey begins with the first step. You personify strength and courage when you live authentically. You must learn to persevere and keep yourself motivated. Always start with a plan and follow it all the way. Don't give up. Rome wasn't built in a day, and similarly your lofty goals won't be realized overnight. You may think your dreams are hopeless at times. Do not give up in the middle of

your journey. Stay the course. There's a strong probability that success could be right around the corner when you're about to give up. Always remember to set realistic goals and follow through on them. No matter how challenging your journey may be, always be willing to stick with it. No matter how often you have been turned down for a job, don't give up. Also, remember to ensure that your expectations are realistic, and your goals are attainable.

4. **Face your fears.** Stop waiting to apply for a promotion until you are more self-assured. Stop turning down opportunities to return to school or learn a new skill. Stop delaying your goals. Start by confronting your anxieties. Everyone occasionally struggles with fear. Some concerns may even serve a purpose by inspiring you to strive harder or push your boundaries. However, if your fears hinder you from taking the necessary steps to ensure your happiness and well-being, it's time to break free. Fearing a little is expected. In actuality, fear aids in your natural defense mechanisms. In the short term, avoiding the circumstances you fear could help you feel better, but avoidance will lead to a life of regret. Practice tackling some of your fears that are brought on by inexperience or uncomfortability. If your dream does not scare you, then it's probably not a dream. Fear keeps you humble because you recognize your humanity. Let your fear propel you forward versus keeping you stuck.

5. **Surround yourself with positive people.** Everybody makes mistakes. Learn from your past mistakes and do better. Do not dwell on them. Also, do not surround yourself with people that use every opportunity to remind you of your mistakes. Whatever your identity, the people you associate with reveal a lot about you. You can be lifted or brought down by the friends you choose. Select friends who are upbeat, ambitious, and encouraging. These are the individuals who will aid in your success. Have supportive friends and be a supportive friend also.

6. **Stay passionate.** One of the best ways to stay motivated is to be passionate about your work. As a result, if you are passionate about what you do, you are more likely to succeed because you will be able to maintain your motivation. You will have an optimistic outlook when you are passionate about your work. You'll practice more. You'll strive to perform better. You won't give up, and your resolve will be greater.

Most importantly, you will adopt an optimistic outlook and develop the conviction that, with effort, everything will work out for the best. This is how extraordinary individuals succeed. They are disciplined and enthusiastic about what they do. And this is the reason they are prosperous.

7. **Learn how to say no.** While doing what you're skilled in can enhance your self-assurance, it's equally

crucial to be aware of circumstances that might make you lose confidence. Perhaps you discover that you feel worse when you engage in a particular activity rather than feeling better about yourself. It's acceptable to decline engagements that undermine your mental well-being. You shouldn't ignore anything that makes you uncomfortable because discomfort is frequently a necessary component of personal development. However, there is nothing wrong with setting boundaries and observing them. Setting limits in social and emotional areas makes you feel psychologically safe.

Additionally, it could make you feel more in control. Feeling in charge of your life is a crucial component of self-worth—boundaries aid in creating a sense of control. Learn the art of saying no. No is a complete sentence when you learn how to slay in your own lane.

8. **Stay humble.** Be honorable in your actions. Success does not come easily. It requires hard work. Be considerate and sympathetic to others as you climb the corporate ladder. You never know when you'll need their assistance. Leadership is when people *choose* to follow you in the absence of power and authority because they believe in you and the vision you are leading. Be a person that people want to follow and intentionally choose. Your humanity is an expression and testament in how you treat people. Always stay humble and remember your journey.

9. **It's acceptable to fail.** When it comes to learning how to slay in your lane, this is your most crucial lesson. The number of times you fail in life doesn't matter. How frequently you get up after failing serves as the yardstick. Keep in mind that failures are learning opportunities. Get back up and prepare for another journey without making the same mistakes again. Failure merely indicates that you were a little bit closer to perfection than you had been before.

10. **Abandon self-sabotage** (Negative Self-Talk). Given that your authentic rhythm has been awakened, you may think or feel doubts about your life more often than in the past. This is the time to practice thinking positive thoughts instead of negative ones. What you say to yourself daily and what you believe about yourself are examples of self-talk. When we talk negatively to ourselves, we may say things like, "This isn't right for someone like me," or "I don't deserve this," or "I can't do this." We are more inclined to act in ways that promote poor self-perceptions when experiencing unpleasant thoughts or sensations about ourselves. Start praising yourself for your abilities, successes, and accomplishments, no matter how big or small. Listen to upbeat music to shift your mindset and create positive vibes!

11. **Use constructive self-talk.** By persuading your subconscious that you can't handle something or that it is too hard, and you shouldn't even try,

negative self-talk can restrict your abilities and lower your self-confidence. On the other hand, positive self-talk can encourage self-compassion, assist in overcoming self-doubt, and encourage you to take on new challenges. Remember that your views aren't always accurate. The next time you feel like you have no business speaking up in a meeting or that your opinions are irrelevant, stop the music. Change the song and beat. Then figure out a strategy to transform those thoughts into more encouraging self-talk and use your voice.

Rhythm Check:

1. How are you composing the rhythm in your life?
2. What is your theme song if your life were an album?
3. What tips for Slaying in Your Lane will you activate starting today?
4. What tip will be hard for you to activate and why? Make sure to discuss this tip with your mentor or accountability partner to help you stay in your lane and win.

Chapter 13: Your Voice is Your Superpower

"To keep on going, you have to keep up the rhythm."
—Haruki Murakami

YOUR VOICE IS YOUR SUPERPOWER

Striving for success in corporate America has come with a cost for many women and minorities. I've heard countless stories of struggle, challenges with being accepted, and feeling as if one doesn't belong. We place so much concern on what "leadership" thinks that we fail to understand that our voice is a differentiator for innovation. Our presence is the beginning of the turning point the corporation greatly needs.

Women aim to be discovered and make an impact. Some women have never known what it means to find their voice. They have not experienced the power of self-belief and proclamation because they have lived believing their role is

"The world is ready,
and women can do it."
—Joy Fitzgerald

about silence, submission, and subservience. Wrong! You can be submissive to authority AND use your voice—subordinate but not subdued. You can choose to be silent but not silenced because you were born to be opinionated and purposeful.

Oprah Winfrey says it this way, "What I know for sure is that speaking your truth is the most powerful tool we all have."

Authentic Rhythm is about discovering your original and genuine voice, not some posh tone the world expects you to exude, but your voice and your truth. For a long time, I feared my voice might be too bold and raw for the world to listen to, especially in corporate America. I remember several occasions when I would get cold feet and cower in my authentic voice.

I remember a time I was preparing to present to our Board of Directors. There were essential things we needed to get approved. I had been feverishly working on my presentation and felt confident about the direction we were taking.

I got a call from my boss that he wanted to meet before the meeting to check in on a few things. In the spirit of being overly prepared, I worked all night to provide as much background material as needed to ensure he was confident we were ready.

I walked into his office with folders falling over me as I printed out too many documents for the dialogue. I sat down and began to pull out and organize all the papers I'd brought in preparation for the conversation. Martin looked at me and said, "Well, Joy, I don't need to talk to you about the content of your presentation. You are always more than prepared. You are one of the best presenters I've heard. No one ever wants to come behind you in the lineup of presentations. I want to talk to you about something different."

I replied, "Okay," but in my mind, I was wondering, *"Where is this going?"* I felt he was about to say something that would make me angry because he struggled to get his point out.

"Joy, you know you are a Black woman, right?"

I nodded my head.

Okay, now he is about to cross the line. Lord, please guide my face and let it not show how I feel. Calm my spirit and give me the wisdom of how to respond to this man. And dear Lord, please don't let him say something disrespectful.

Martin continued. "And you are the only Black woman in this meeting. And sometimes being a Black woman in a room full of White men can be somewhat uncomfortable and maybe a little intimidating, so I need you to go out of your way to make them comfortable so they can hear you."

I replied more slowly, "Ohhhhh kayyyyyy?" with a slight question mark at the end.

"So, to ensure that you are successful, make sure you talk with a smile. Smiling while you are talking can make you appear less aggressive."

Wait, did he just say that?

Did he just ask me to smile and reduce my presence so that my skin color wouldn't make them feel intimidated? Breathe Joy.

"Oh, and one more thing, I really like it when your hair is straight. That's a good look on you, very professional."

Facetiously, I asked, "Should we talk about what I should wear to appear less manly, given that I am a Black woman?"

He missed the hint and excitedly responded, "Yes, that is a great idea! You shouldn't wear a pants suit. That might come off as too manly. I suggest wearing a dress."

Now I am mortified and hurt.

"So, Joy, make sure you practice talking with a smile, got it? Other than that, I think we are good. Oh, and by the way, if they ask you any questions, look at me first. If I nod my head, then you can answer. Otherwise, I will answer all the questions."

I responded, "Sure, Martin. Can I ask you a question? Have you ever been told to smile when you deliver a presentation to appear less threatening? And have you ever given this coaching to men?"

Stunned, Martin said, "Well, I don't have to give men this advice because they are the norm. You are the exception. Your gender and race combined might be a trigger for some in the room. So, I am just trying to help *you* be successful. Trust me. I am helping you!"

Martin then paused for what felt like hours, but it was actually more like seconds. He said, "I can't honestly think of a time when I gave this advice to a man or that I was given this advice. I am a little embarrassed to admit this but while this is hard to share, I am trying to protect you. I hope you know that."

This is the experience of so many women. I believe we all have experienced a Martin in our careers. My question to you is: Who is your Martin?

A "Martin" is a person that either propels or stifles your authentic rhythm and your dreams. For this section, the term Martin is neither male nor female. Martin represents all people and all demographics. I want to introduce four types of people we will affectionally refer to as Martin.

1. Martin the Dream Killer
2. Martin the Dream Stealer
3. Martin the Dream Weaver
4. Martin the Dream Builder

Let's meet Martin the dream killer. When I first decided I wanted to write a book, I called Martin the dream killer. I was so excited about the opportunity to share my dream with Martin (I didn't know they were a dream killer or maybe I secretly did but hoped they wouldn't be this time.) I shared, "I am going to write a book. I have been thinking about this for years and now I finally have the courage to do it."

Martin the dream killer said, "Why would you do that? You don't have time for that. You barely have enough time to do all the things currently on your plate. Why would you want to take on more? Plus, what would your job say? Do you really want to expose yourself to the world? I don't think it's a good idea. Trust me, you'll regret it. But don't ask me. Do whatever you think is best. I just don't think it's a good idea!"

Have you ever called someone excited about an idea and by the time you are done listening to their opinions, you've lost confidence in your idea? By the time I was done listening to Martin the dream killer, they had sucked up every bit of energy, joy, and happiness I had in writing the book! They made me second-guess my dream. I left the conversation questioning my ability to write the book and my desire seemed unattainable and frivolous.

I pondered, *why would I take on something so ambitious? That's a lot of work. Is it worth it? Will I be good at it? Can I find the time? Will anyone buy or read my book? Do I have anything to say that is worth sharing? What if I fail?*

Has there ever been an idea or something you wanted to pursue and Martin the dream killer made you lose faith in yourself? Martin could be your spouse, best friend, parent, leader, sibling, children, boss, or coworker. Dream killers will deplete your emotional energy in believing in yourself. They pour negativity and toxicity on all your dreams and goals. They are the reason most innovative ideas are never realized. First, recognize the person as a dream killer and once you do, stop sharing your dreams with them.

Dream killers don't believe in dreams because no one believes in their dreams. It may also be that they haven't accomplished their dreams. They lack the capacity, capability, and experience to help you build your dream because no one helped them. In most cases, they don't mean to be negative, but they are, and you need to recognize who they are in your life.

Here are a few common ways to identify Martin the dream killer. These are the Martinisms you might hear:

- I am a realist, so I am just telling you the truth.
- I am a glass half-empty type of person and that's how the world really is.
- You don't have time to pursue that job or goal.
- You should just be satisfied with what you have.
- You waited too late to dream.
- Why would you want to put that type of stress on yourself?
- You know it's going to be really hard, so are you sure you want to do this?
- If I was you, I would just be happy with the job I have.
- Why go after that promotion? You won't get it anyway so why even try?

Martin the dream killer will crush your dreams and aspirations. They will cause you to be confused and second-guess the very thing you should be doing. Ditch the perfect plan and do what feels right in your soul. What makes sense to you may not make sense to others and that's because it's your dream, not theirs.

Never share your dreams with dream killers. They don't deserve the permission to pour into your mindset. In fact, they have more opinions on what everyone else should be doing versus themselves. They are the critics of your family, workplaces, and communities. They can be counted on to deplete and kill dreams. Who are the Martins in your life that are killing your dreams?

Only share your career goals, dreams, and aspirations with people that have the capacity, ability, and experience to help you activate your ambitions. If they don't have those things, they are not worthy to have input into your dreams!

Next, let's meet Martin the dream stealer. This Martin comes to work every day in pursuit of stealing the dreams, ideas, and innovations of others. Martin could be your peer, team member, or even your boss. Martin loves to ask questions in pursuit of knowledge. Unfortunately, one thing that is certain about this Martin—they can be counted on to take the ideas of others and claim them as their own.

I remember one day coming up with an exciting idea to pitch a new communications strategy. Since Martin was always friendly and open to meeting with me, I decided to test my idea with them. Martin began to ask several detailed questions about my approach. I was naïve and thought Martin was really trying to understand to better offer help and support. Martin the dream stealer then began to tell me why it "potentially" couldn't work. Martin didn't necessarily kill the dream but left me wondering if I needed to invest more time and work prior to pitching the idea.

Later that week during staffing, my leader looked at Martin excitedly and asked them to share their great idea with the team. Martin then proceeded to share MY IDEA! Stunned, I could barely compose my disappointment and hurt. Martin even had the audacity to begin their pitch by saying, "I was talking with Joy earlier this week about an idea." Martin the dream stealer then had the nerve to come up to me after the meeting and state, "Joy wasn't that great? They absolutely loved the idea! I knew you were a little skittish about it so I figured I would help you get it over the fence and take ownership. Now you don't have to worry about feeling accountable. I will take it on from here and you get the benefit of knowing your idea helped us." Wow!

Corporate America has its share of dream stealers. These are individuals that will listen to your ideas and try to take credit for them. Time and time again, ideas are brought into the workplace only to have Martin the dream stealer take credit for their innovative perspectives. They will try to beat you to the punch. Have you ever shared with a colleague that you were going to apply for a new job or promotion to learn that they applied only after learning of your interest to apply? Be on alert for Martin the dream stealer.

Now let's meet Martin the dream weaver. This Martin is very necessary to have in your life. They are the coaches, counselors, and individuals that help you think differently. They offer sage advice and wisdom in helping you assess if your dream is real or attainable. They help you understand the potential pathways or avenues needed to activate your dream. They help you weave and thread your dream into a reality by helping you see vantage points you might not have seen without their advice.

Martin the dream killer is a person that has advice or great questions only. They don't actually *do* anything to help you, but they have great insight that is helpful and critical in realizing your dreams. Martin the dream weaver might be known by others as a great coach or referred to as a great listener. They are willing to avail their thought leadership in helping you.

I remember a critical time in my career when I needed advice. I was offered a role that was outside of my core skills and competencies. The role was highly visible to senior leadership and had a great deal of room for failure. It was new and had never been done before inside the organization. I didn't have the experience, but I had transferable skills. I called Martin the dream weaver and asked for their thoughts on the opportunity. Martin the dream weaver helped me understand both the risks and the opportunities. They left me better prepared to make the decision that would help me propel my career. Here are a few benefits of having a Martin the dream weaver:

- They help you understand both the risk and opportunities of your dreams or decisions.
- They believe in you and help you to think holistically about your situation.
- They are encouragers while also realistic.
- They are great listeners and help you feel heard and not judged.
- You leave the conversation feeling inspired but also more inquisitive.
- Your ideas, dreams, and career aspirations are valued, and you feel supported by them.
- They offer you psychological safely as they never undermine your dreams or aspirations.
- They can be trusted to not steal your ideas.
- They ask questions that help YOU arrive at the decisions you need to make.

Who are the Martins that will help you weave your dreams?

The last person is Martin the dream builder. Dr. Martin Luther King, Jr. is the ultimate dream builder. He had a powerful persona that helped shape America in realizing the civil liberties we now enjoy. He is the quintessential Martin the dream builder that helped a nation to imagine a future that never existed. He helped usher in an era that brought unification and love to a lost generation. Living in your authentic rhythm requires a Martin the dream builder.

A dream builder is a person that not only believes in you but helps activate your dream. They take dream weaving one step further. They are willing to get active, involved, and engaged in helping you ignite your dream or your vision. They can be counted on to extend their resources, relationship capital, time, and talents to help make your dream possible. They ask, "What do you need?"

When I called Martin the dream builder to talk about my first book, I left the conversation not only inspired but with a plan of activation. They identified ways in which they could offer both help and support. They were as excited about the dream as me. They offered support and advice for every risk we identified. They promised to also serve as my accountability partner because they recognized it would get hard and at times, the dream would feel daunting. They knew that in those times, I would need encouragement and emotional support.

This helped me understand and evaluate success and winning on MY terms. They ensured I understood what it meant to slay in my lane. They encouraged me to avoid comparing myself with others but rather define my own criteria and terms for success. They allowed me to envision my dream through the lens of a Martin the dream builder. They didn't shrink my dream, they actually made it bigger.

The most powerful question a dream builder will ask is, how can I help you? And they meet you in the intersection of your dreams, possibilities, and aspirations. They bring energy to the conversation because they too can envision a reality that hasn't yet occurred. Everyone needs a Martin the dream builder.

Who are your Martins that build dreams and who are you being a Martin the dream builder for?

In many cases, our dream builders aren't those who we might want or expect them to be. They may not be those closest to you. It's all right. The universe has provided all that you need to activate your dreams if you are willing to be present enough to see the Martins in your life and vulnerable enough to ask for help. Use your voice and reach out to your Martin the dream builder.

In dealing with all Martins, your voice is your superpower so how are you using it? You must speak truth to power and hold power accountable to the truth.

Regardless of what change of tempo or beat life brings your way, don't stop using your voice, and don't diminish your femininity. Women have believed we need to be submissive and docile because of our feminine nature. Women are supporters, not leaders, some audaciously say. How dare a woman has an opinion. These societal beliefs have been ingrained from our days as little girls. People mistakenly believe that women must have a tough-as-nails attitude to succeed, especially in workplaces where men dominate. Emotion, passion, and compassion are vital qualities that shouldn't be discounted or kept secret at work.

Be yourself and not a modified version of yourself. Learn to walk in your light and speak your truth to the world. Be your own biggest fan!

Women who succeed are conscious of both their skills

and flaws. Know that you are priceless and precious from the top of your head to the soles of your feet. Your voice is a tool that can be utilized to speak up for what is right instead of what is convenient. With a voice, you have a forum for your thoughts and the chance to gain insight and understanding about important issues. Every voice is unique and has a special message to convey. Voices can create change. Your voice is one of the few things that cannot be taken away if you use it. The purpose of voices is to join and support one another by uplifting other voices.

Since the beginning, women have been seen as the caring gender, trapped between where she believes she should be and where society thinks she should be. She plays so many parts and frequently falls short of fulfilling them.

Choices about balancing work and life have effects. It's okay to admit that you can't accomplish everything on your own and a bit of assistance might help lessen your enormous workload. Be fully present wherever you are and pay attention to everyone around you, whether coworkers, customers, or family members at home. Every woman has a voice that can be translated into deeds that make the world and workplace better.

Take pride in your femininity. Embrace the divine feminine that resides within you. Women often discount their intuition, reflecting how their culture taught them. In reality, the Divine Feminine is a potent force. It is not merely an idea or concept. The energy that generates life is Divine Energy. Women are caregivers and warriors. So, start caring for yourself. Nurture your dreams. Fulfill your career aspirations. Share your ideas and use your voice. Above all, embrace your inner woman and love her *unapologetically.*

Rhythm Check: ♪ 🥁

1. How do you use your voice in your organization?
2. Who are the Martins in your life? Who do you need to stop sharing your dreams with?
3. How have you muted your voice due to fear?
4. How can you use your voice to support others that are different from you?
5. How can you make an impact to advocate for underrepresented populations?

CONCLUSION

You are a work of music. You are wonderfully created to live the best authentic version of yourself. Be you!

You can attain new heights in every aspect of your life by having faith in yourself. You are worth the work and effort the path to greatness requires. Picture your ideal life and put forth the effort and persevere to realize your career objectives. Changing your thinking is work, but the results are worthwhile. So, why are you still waiting? Start pursuing your goals and go after the career you've always wanted. You can do this! With all your might, follow your dreams and become unstoppable! Go for the next promotion, apply for the job you've always wanted, go back to college, or take a new class to learn a new skill.

Success is not dependent on perfection. It depends on taking chances, working hard, and never giving up. The journey is not easy, and it comes with many challenges, setbacks, and disappointments. However, the journey becomes so much easier when you stop trying to be something that you are not and live authentically! On the road to success, you will make mistakes; expect it. Mistakes are proof that you tried, and they are necessary for giving you the proper conditioning to succeed. You are capable and possess the ability to win on YOUR terms!

If you don't spend time with yourself, figuring out who you are and what gives you fulfillment, no one—not a life coach or counselor—can provide the answers you are desperately seeking.

What's going to give you fulfillment? Only you can give yourself that answer, but you must engage in self-discovery to unearth and bring to light the mysteries of your life. When you have done the self-work outlined in the previous chapters, you will be more confident in your solutions and better equipped to achieve your career and life goals. And don't be afraid of what answers you find. Walk in faith and truth as you find those answers.

Women our struggles in life and corporate America are real, palpable, legitimate, and undeniable. Every day, many women face microinequities, macro-inequities, misogyny, misappropriation, and imposter syndrome. We question whether we are good enough. We contemplate whether we can achieve our aspirations. We ask ourselves if we should desire success or whether we can be as successful as men. We secretly doubt they will give us a chance.

Women, we are strong, resilient, talented, powerful, capable, and READY! If our jobs aren't taxing enough, we must question things that extend far beyond the job or role. We face many decisions that come with judgment relative to our authentic feminine nature. Things such as how we wear our hair, how we dress, our style, and the list goes on and on and on.

Here are some of the things women contemplate daily, should we color our hair, and will the color be "work" appropriate? Should we wear a dress, or will pants better represent a leader persona? What is the work-appropriate length of our dresses or skirts? Wait…if you are tall, most dresses appear shorter. We wonder if we will be taken seriously if we wear our hair curly versus straight. We privately wonder but are too fearful to ask, are hoop earrings appropriate for work, or is it more appropriate to wear a conservative, classic pair of diamond studs? We wonder if we can wear bright colors on our fingernails and what messages might be associated with the length of our nails. Should we wear pantyhose or not? We wonder if we are too curvy or shapely to wear certain apparel to work. We question if we will be taken seriously if we appear too feminine. Should we tell the company that we are pregnant or getting married? How will having a baby impact career opportunities to excel in the organization? What if I have to take off because my baby is sick? What will the company think of me? Women face these questions every day and so many more.

The proverbial corporate ceiling still exists in every industry for many populations. The corporate journey can seem arduous, onerous, and difficult to navigate. Some may even feel that, at times, it challenges your femininity. Every day, we must make it our responsibility to change the course and journey for women all over the world. We must confront our fears and live in our truth. We must not become fatigued or exasperated but rather empowered to show the world that we are here and deserve to be respected, valued, welcomed, and heard. We must support other women and minority populations to help them thrive so that they can win on their terms.

Yes, you can find your beat, dance to your rhythm, and slay in your lane. Stay focused, fearless, resilient, and committed. Protect your time, guard your heart, reflect to preserve your mindset, and be intentional in standing out on purpose. Don't bury your talents, shrink your voice, and give up your authentic rhythm. You can achieve your dreams and have fun trying. Either way, learning and growing is winning.

Don't allow what others think to obliterate your career aspirations. When I stopped trying not to sound Southern, when I wore what made me feel confident at work, when I started using my voice in meetings, and when I started learning how to engage in small talk to connect with others, I found my authentic rhythm and won on my terms. I was the most successful in my career when I lived my authentic rhythm.

Every one of us has a tiny drum that beats in our hearts to direct us toward life's path that will nourish us the most. It can be challenging to listen to your inner voice or your inner drum. You must be prepared to follow your path if you want to be successful. We long for new directions, fresh starts, and new opportunities. When you start listening to your drum, you will feel liberated and empowered to pursue your passion. You must live your life on your terms if you want to find true fulfillment. You must compose your music, play your instruments, and dance to the beat of your soul's melody.

I am on a continual journey to live my authentic rhythm. I try to live it out loud so that people see and feel it. I hope that I am contagiously encouraging and inspiring others to find their purpose and live it authentically.

I'm still a work in progress. But one thing I know is my purpose and my "why" in life. I know my divine assignment and that my gift is to speak joy into the hearts, minds, and souls of everyone I'm honored to meet. I hope I have ignited a fire in you that lets you know a dream, an aspiration, or a vision is not age dependent. It is dependent on YOU! As long as there is breath in your body, there is the ability, and there is still that appointment for you to sing and dance your authentic rhythm in this beautiful and amazing gift we all enjoy called life.

I hope you find your authentic rhythm and achieve all that life has to offer. I wish you success in obtaining your career goals and aspirations. It has been my pleasure. It has been my privilege. Until next time.

ACKNOWLEDGMENTS

This book is a journey that I feel blessed and honored to share with each of you. Writing a book is one of the most vulnerable steps one will take in exposing oneself to the world. What started out as a proclamation on stage in Las Vegas ultimately changed the course of my life for the last ten months. I took the opportunity to make my lifelong dream of writing this book a reality. It is because of readers like you that I get to live my purpose.

Let me first begin by telling anyone who has a desire to write a book, to be sure that this is *your* dream. This process is long and arduous and requires many sacrifices. You will not accomplish this goal alone. It will require the tireless efforts of a fantastic team!

Let me introduce you to my team. My team begins with my daughter, Taylor. I am grateful to be the mother of two phenomenal children, each holds a special place and purpose in my life. Taylor is my creative genius, and she has the gift of ideation. In most cases, she was the first person with whom I shared book ideas. I am grateful for her innovative insights that helped to make this book different and creative.

Your sage advice helped me try new things and think outside the box. I also must give her credit for some of the spiffy quotes in the book.

To my mother, Ann, who is the best dream builder a person could ever have in life. She not only encouraged me, she was willing to get active and help in the process. Mom, thanks for the first edits and pre-reads, no matter the day, time, or hour. The countless phone calls not only kept me going, they encouraged me.

Thanks to my son, Tyron, for serving as my emotional well-being coach. You always made sure I had balance and didn't take the task of writing too seriously. You always found a way to help me reframe my mindset and focus on what I could control. You brought the son-shine during this process.

To my husband, Tyron Sr., words seem inadequate to express how pivotal you are to this book. You have been the wind beneath my wings. You selflessly gave up our time together so I could engage in the rigorous writing process. You pushed me to rewrite and go deeper even when I wanted to stop. Babe, because of you, I am a better me, and I have given my best to this project!

To my publisher, Renita, and the outstanding team at Mynd Matters Publishing, thank you for your excellence. Your brilliant advice and soft coaching have made this process pleasant and stress-free. Detreich, thanks for your patience as I came up with new ideas and requests at the last minute. You always made me feel valued and heard.

To Marissa, Joelle, and the entire team at Smith Publicity, you far exceeded expectations. I can't think of a better team to work with.

Thanks to my family and all of my amazing friends for your continued support. To my sister Kristy, thanks for your advice and for being the little sister who always wants to help. Thanks to my best friend Dee for your support and for throwing the best book launch party ever.

I want to send a special thanks to all the organizations, corporations, women's groups, foundations, and any organization that has invited me to speak and share my journey.

To everyone who has ever purchased any of my books, sent a kind message, or followed my journey—it is because of you that I get to live out my ultimate purpose in speaking joy.

ABOUT THE AUTHOR

JOY FITZGERALD currently serves as the Senior Vice President, Chief Diversity, Equity, and Inclusion Officer of UnitedHealth Group. She is a global business executive and respected thought leader. Joy is one of the nation's most respected voices on diversity as a business strategy. She has been featured in numerous publications including *Harvard Business Review, Fortune Magazine, The Wall Street Journal, The New York Times, The Insider, Black Enterprise, Gallup,* and *Profiles in Diversity Journal.*

She is an organizational strategist who has dedicated her career to improving the lives of individuals, one person at a time. She has been a leader in both the private and public sectors. Prior to joining UnitedHealth Group, Joy served as the Vice President Human Resources and Chief Diversity & Inclusion Officer of Eli Lilly and Company. As the leader of Global Diversity, Equity, and Inclusion, Joy partners with business leaders to attract and develop talent, increase health equity outcomes, make a societal impact, and grow the business. Known as an inspirational leader, Joy has a rare ability to tackle difficult subjects and speak truth to power without stirring negative emotions. She is skillful and experienced in translating diversity, equity and inclusion into business solutions that address both business and people challenges. Joy is influential in connecting both the head (intellectual) and heart (emotional) in a strategic way that transforms organizational culture.

Joy has more than twenty-five years of leadership experience working across business sectors in various industries. She is a highly sought-after executive coach helping leaders go from where they are to where they aspire to be. As a dynamic speaker and strategic thought partner, Joy has presented keynote speeches and workshops in more than twenty-five countries across five continents. She has served on boards and received numerous awards and recognition for her work in being a disruptive leader who is making a difference in corporate America.

She was named by *Diversity Journal* as a "Woman Worth Watching," by Healthcare Businesswomen's Association as a "Rising Star," inducted by Color in the Inaugural Power List of 50 Chief Diversity Officers, and by Black Enterprise as a Top Executive in Corporate Diversity and Most Powerful Woman in Corporate Diversity.

Joy is an accomplished leader who works tirelessly to champion inclusion by creating safe spaces for brave conversations on topics of injustice and inequities. She has led major transformative business strategies, built marketing immersive strategies, and developed global training curriculums. Her work has been cited in several top publications as best practices.

She has authored two books, *The Journey to Joy: 5 Generations Share Stories Every Woman Needs to Hear* and *The Journal to Joy.*

Printed in the USA
CPSIA information can be obtained
at www.ICGtesting.com
CBHW031434300923
1186CB00001B/3